David Bejou, PhD
Adrian Palmer, PhD
Editors

The Future of Relationship Marketing

The Future of Relationship Marketing has been co-published simultaneously as *Journal of Relationship Marketing*, Volume 4, Numbers 3/4 2005.

Pre-publication REVIEWS, COMMENTARIES, EVALUATIONS . . .

"**I**F YOU ARE INTERESTED IN RE-LATIONSHIP MARKETING THIS IS THE BOOK FOR YOU. The seven contributions that comprise the book provide a broad overview of the field. The extensive references serve as a source for further research."

David T. Wilson, PhD, MBA
Clemens Professor of Marketing Emeritus
Pennsylvania State University

More pre-publication
REVIEWS, COMMENTARIES, EVALUATIONS . . .

"The business community is asking questions about how a relationship can be created and maintained. What should the economics of a relationship look like? Is CRM the whole answer or just a part of it? This book is a long overdue meeting point where THE PROBLEMS OF IMPLEMENTATION ARE EXPLICITLY ADDRESSED to provide both sound theoretical exposition and clear understanding and guidance."

Mark Gabbott, PhD
Professor of Marketing
Monash University

BEST
BUSINESS
BOOKS

Best Business Books®
An Imprint of The Haworth Press, Inc.

The Future
of Relationship Marketing

The Future of Relationship Marketing has been co-published simultaneously as *Journal of Relationship Marketing,* Volume 4, Numbers 3/4 2005.

Monographic Separates from the *Journal of Relationship Marketing*™

For additional information on these and other Haworth Press titles, including descriptions, tables of contents, reviews, and prices, use the QuickSearch catalog at http://www.HaworthPress.com.

The Future of Relationship Marketing, edited by David Bejou, PhD, and Adrian Palmer, PhD, (Vol. 4, No. 3/4, 2005). *"If you are interested in relationship marketing THIS IS THE BOOK FOR YOU." (David T. Wilson, PhD, MBA, Clemens Professor of Marketing, Emeritus, Pennsylvania State University)*

Internal Relationship Management: Linking Human Resources to Marketing Performance, edited by Michael D. Hartline, PhD, and David Bejou, PhD (Vol. 3, No. 2/3, 2004). *"FINALLY, there is a scholarly book on internal employee relationship management. . . . Links human resources to marketing performance." (Jagdish N. Sheth, PhD, Charles H. Kellstadt Professor of Marketing, Emory University)*

Customer Relationship Management in Electronic Markets, edited by Gopalkrishnan R. Iyer, PhD, and David Bejou, PhD (Vol. 2, No. 3/4, 2003). *"Extremely helpful for business people and university faculty. I RECOMMEND THIS BOOK HIGHLY." (James E. Littlefield, PhD, Professor of Marketing, Virginia Polytechnic Institute and State University, Blacksburg)*

The Future of Relationship Marketing

David Bejou, PhD
Adrian Palmer, PhD
Editors

The Future of Relationship Marketing has been co-published simultaneously as *Journal of Relationship Marketing*, Volume 4, Numbers 3/4 2005.

Best Business Books®
An Imprint of The Haworth Press, Inc.

New York • London • Victoria (AU)
www.HaworthPress.com

Published by

The Best Business Books®, 10 Alice Street, Binghamton, NY 13904-1580 USA

The Best Business Books® is an imprint of The Haworth Press, Inc., 10 Alice Street, Binghamton, NY 13904-1580 USA.

The Future of Relationship Marketing has been co-published simultaneously as *Journal of Relationship Marketing*, Volume 4, Numbers 3/4 2005.

Cover design by Christie R. Peterson

Library of Congress Cataloging-in-Publication Data

The future of relationship marketing / David Bejou, Adrian Palmer, editors.
    p. cm.
"Co-published simultaneously as Journal of relationship marketing, Volume 4, Numbers 3/4 2005."
ISBN-13: 978-0-7890-3161-7 (hard cover : alk. paper)
ISBN-10: 0-7890-3161-2 (hard cover : alk. paper)
ISBN-13: 978-0-7890-3162-4 (soft cover : alk. paper)
ISBN-10: 0-7890-3162-0 (soft cover : alk. paper)
    1. Relationship marketing. 2. Customer relations. 3. Marketing. I. Bejou, David. II. Palmer, Adrian. III. Journal of relationship marketing (Binghamton, N.Y.)

HF5415.55.F88 2006
658.8'12–dc22

2005021081

Indexing, Abstracting & Website/Internet Coverage

This section provides you with a list of major indexing & abstracting services and other tools for bibliographic access. That is to say, each service began covering this periodical during the year noted in the right column. Most Websites which are listed below have indicated that they will either post, disseminate, compile, archive, cite or alert their own Website users with research-based content from this work. (This list is as current as the copyright date of this publication.)

Abstracting, Website/Indexing Coverage . . . . Year When Coverage Began

- *ABI/INFORM Global. Contents of this publication are indexed and abstracted in the ABI/INFORM Global database, available on ProQuest Information & Learning @ www.proquest.com* **2001**
- *ABI/INFORM Research. Contents of this publication are indexed and abstracted in the ABI/INFORM Research database, available on ProQuest Information & Learning @ www.proquest.com* . . . **2001**
- *BEFO <http://www.fiz-technik.de/en_db/d_befo.htm>* **2003**
- *EBSCOhost Electronic Journals Service (EJS) <http://ejournals.ebsco.com>* **2002**
- *ELMAR (Current Table of Contents Services) American Marketing Assn <http://www.elmar-list.org/>* **2001**
- *Elsevier Scopus <http://www.info.scopus.com>* **2005**
- *Foods Adlibra* **2001**
- *Google <http://www.google.com>* **2004**
- *Google Scholar <http://scholar.google.com>* **2004**
- *Haworth Document Delivery Center <http://www.HaworthPress.com/journals/dds.asp>* **2002**
- *Human Resources Abstracts (HRA)* **2001**
- *IBZ International Bibliography of Periodical Literature <http://www.saur.de>* **2002**

(continued)

Special Bibliographic Notes related to special journal issues (separates) and indexing/abstracting:

- indexing/abstracting services in this list will also cover material in any "separate" that is co-published simultaneously with Haworth's special thematic journal issue or DocuSerial. Indexing/abstracting usually covers material at the article/chapter level.
- monographic co-editions are intended for either non-subscribers or libraries which intend to purchase a second copy for their circulating collections.
- monographic co-editions are reported to all jobbers/wholesalers/approval plans. The source journal is listed as the "series" to assist the prevention of duplicate purchasing in the same manner utilized for books-in-series.
- to facilitate user/access services all indexing/abstracting services are encouraged to utilize the co-indexing entry note indicated at the bottom of the first page of each article/chapter/contribution.
- this is intended to assist a library user of any reference tool (whether print, electronic, online, or CD-ROM) to locate the monographic version if the library has purchased this version but not a subscription to the source journal.
- individual articles/chapters in any Haworth publication are also available through the Haworth Document Delivery Service (HDDS).

The Future
of Relationship Marketing

CONTENTS

ABOUT THE EDITORS

David Bejou, PhD, is Professor of Marketing and Dean of School of Business at Virginia State University. He previously served on the faculty of the University of North Carolina at Wilmington, where he was nominated in 1996 for the Chancellor Teaching Excellence Award, and nominated in both 1995 and 1996 for the Faculty Scholarship Award. He has also been a faculty member at several other universities in the United States and Australia.

Dr. Bejou has published widely in professional journals, including the *Journal of Services Marketing*, the *Journal of Business Research*, the *Journal of Marketing Management*, the *International Journal of Bank Marketing*, and the *European Journal of Marketing*. He is a member of the American Marketing Association and the Academy of Marketing Science, and has been a presenter or Session Chair at many national and international conferences.

Dr. Bejou has served as a marketing/promotions consultant to the United Carolina Bank (UCB), Brunswick Community College, and other businesses and community organizations.

Adrian Palmer, PhD, is Professor of Services Marketing at the University of Gloucestershire, Cheltenham, UK. Previously, he created the Centre for Tourism Marketing at the University of Ulster, Northern Ireland. Before joining academia, he held management positions within the travel and transport industries. He is a Fellow of the Chartered Institute of Marketing and a Chartered Marketer.

Dr. Palmer is the author of 7 books and over 50 journal articles, which have focused on aspects of buyer-seller relationships within the services sector, especially tourism. He is a member of the editorial advisory board for *Journal of Relationship Marketing*, *European Journal of Marketing*, *Journal of Marketing Management* and *Journal of Services Marketing*.

Dr. Palmer has completed several major consultancy projects, focusing on marketing activities of public and private sector tourism related organisations.

Preface

Welcome to the 2005 special edition of the *Journal of Relationship Marketing*. This special edition is based on the proceedings of the 11th Annual Colloquium in Relationship Marketing, held at Cheltenham, UK. This was the gathering of some of the leading academics who have been associated with the development of Relationship Marketing. The conference seemed timely, in view of the growing depth and breadth of theory about buyer-seller relationships, set alongside a sometimes skeptical audience of businesses who may not have seen the pay off from relationship development, and consumers for whom relationships may be unsought. I am very thankful to all of the individuals who made this special issue a success.

If you are interested in becoming an ad hoc reviewer for *JRM*, please send or email a brief statement indicating your areas of expertise and interest along with a copy of your CV. I would like to encourage you and your colleagues to consider submitting your research and your proposal for special editions to *JRM*. Please contact me if you have any questions. Comments and suggestions are always welcome.

Thanks!

David Bejou, PhD
(E-mail: dbejou@vsu.edu)
Professor of Marketing
Dean, School of Business
Virginia State University
Founding Editor, Journal of Relationship Marketing
Senior Editor, Relationship Marketing Books

[Haworth co-indexing entry note]: "Preface." Bejou, David. Co-published simultaneously in *Journal of Relationship Marketing* (Best Business Books, an imprint of The Haworth Press, Inc.) Vol. 4, No. 3/4, 2005, p. xxiii; and: *The Future of Relationship Marketing* (ed: David Bejou, and Adrian Palmer) Best Business Books, an imprint of The Haworth Press, Inc., 2005, p. xi. Single or multiple copies of this article are available for a fee from The Haworth Document Delivery Service [1-800-HAWORTH, 9:00 a.m. - 5:00 p.m. (EST). E-mail address: docdelivery@haworthpress.com].

The Future of Relationship Marketing

Adrian Palmer

Gloucestershire Business School, UK

David Bejou

Virginia State University

This special edition of *Journal of Relationship Marketing* is based on the proceedings of the 11th Annual Colloquium in Relationship Marketing, held at Cheltenham, UK. This saw the gathering of some of the leading academics who have been associated with the development of Relationship Marketing. The conference theme of "Refreshing the Challenge of Relationship Marketing" seemed timely, in view of the growing depth and breadth of theory about buyer-seller relationships, set alongside a sometimes skeptical audience of businesses who may not have seen the pay off from relationship development, and consumers for whom relationships may be unsought.

One of the features of the Colloquium was a motion debate that "Relationship Marketing theories are overstated in relation to their importance to business." The debate sought to focus attention on the continuing quest of marketing academics to develop theories of Relationship Marketing, alongside the sometimes questionable success of attempts to implement the principles.

The motion was vigorously promoted by two proposers and challenged by two opposers. An audience of 54 academics was asked to vote on the motion before and after the debate. On a Likert scale ranging from 1 (strongly disagree) to 5 (strongly agree), the average score before the debate was 4.1. Through the power of debate, this score rose to

[Haworth co-indexing entry note]: "The Future of Relationship Marketing." Palmer, Adrian, and David Bejou. Co-published simultaneously in *Journal of Relationship Marketing* (Best Business Books, an imprint of The Haworth Press, Inc.) Vol. 4, No. 3/4, 2005, pp. 1-10; and: *The Future of Relationship Marketing* (ed: David Bejou, and Adrian Palmer) Best Business Books, an imprint of The Haworth Press, Inc., 2005, pp. 1-10. Single or multiple copies of this article are available for a fee from The Haworth Document Delivery Service [1-800-HAWORTH, 9:00 a.m. - 5:00 p.m. (EST). E-mail address: docdelivery@haworthpress. com].

4.3 when the same measure was taken immediately following the conclusion of the debate, suggesting that leading academics in the field had apparently convinced themselves of the shortcomings of their area of academic specialization.

How could it be that a collection of some of the top academics in the subject could be so critical of the theory base of Relationship Marketing, which they have contributed extensively to? Could the audience have been underplaying the status of the considerable body of theory which Relationship Marketing has developed? Were academics suggesting that Relationship Marketing really isn't of great practical importance to practitioners? Or were they just cynical about the ways in which practitioners had adopted it?

Relationship Marketing has been mutating with subtle changes in language appearing in published material and training courses, for example "Customer Relationship Management," "database marketing," "direct marketing" and "customer loyalty." "Customer experience" appears to be a more recent semantic shift and offers academics an opportunity to integrate the currently disjointed streams of theory on the emotional relationships that individuals have with a brand and the interpersonal relationships that have been the focus for Relationship Marketing. For practitioners, who are increasingly appointing "customer experience managers," the customer experience may lie somewhere between the intellectual over development and operationally under specified field of Relationship Marketing, and the short term, operationally driven customer relationship management.

Like many new ideas within the domain of marketing, Relationship Marketing emerged as a "new" paradigm, only to attract increased critical attention as the assumptions of the emergent paradigm came open to challenge. "Relationship Marketing" has been described as a "popularized buzzword" (Coviello et al., 1997, p 26); while many have criticized the lack of an integrated underlying theory of Relationship Marketing (e.g., Gummeson, 1987). The crucial point is that while relational concepts have become even more firmly embedded in models of buyer behavior, "Relationship Marketing" as an integrating and underpinning conceptual framework has become increasingly challenged. There should be little surprise at this process of emergence and criticism, reflecting Gladwell's model of how new ideas emerge and are subsequently challenged by a new emerging orthodoxy (Gladwell 2000).

Is Relationship Marketing, in the words of Christopher, Payne and Ballantyne an "idea whose time has come" (Christopher, Payne and Ballantyne 1991) or an idea that is approaching its "use by" date? Given the rising level of self-critical introspection by academics and practitioners of Relationship Marketing, now is the time to refresh the challenge of defining relationships within marketing. This special issue of *Journal of Relationship Marketing* presents six of the most thought-provoking papers presented at the colloquium, which each raised important issues about the direction in which Relationship Marketing should develop.

DEFINING A THEORY BASE
FOR RELATIONSHIP MARKETING

One reason for the alleged shortcomings in theories of Relationship Marketing may arise from a focus among many researchers on what Ehrensal (1999) has described as the "science of administration", rather than a critical evaluation of theory. The early development of Relationship Marketing tended to draw mainly–though by no means exclusively–on the extant marketing literature, at the expense of the depth and breadth of literature in sociology and psychology. Wensley (1999) noted that some of the current debates in marketing had occurred in sociology 20 years previously. Some of the most interesting advances in marketing theory have occurred at the borders with other disciplines rather than within the confines of marketing.

The positivist approach to researching buyer-seller relationships–dominant among US researchers–has tended to emphasize the measurement and imputation of values to relationships. This has complemented the European approach, which has tended to conceptualize and seek a deeper understanding of the meaning of marketing relationships. It has been suggested that the positivist tradition of marketing academics–especially within the US–may explain why relatively few academic Relationship Marketing articles have been written from a sociological perspective (Burton, 2001). This special edition combines approaches from both research perspectives.

In their article published in this special issue, Pels and Saren remind us that managers selectively choose, from a jungle of existing theories, those theories that most closely describe their own world views and ideologies. Managers use theories and knowledge claims that are consistent with their own frame of reference, It follows that if we look for relationships in business, what we see may be a social construction based upon our own notion of what a relationship should be.

But what about the notion that Relationship Marketing theories are unimportant to business? Is there an unbridgeable gap between theory and practice? Academic marketers have been accused of 'talking about increasingly narrow issues in an increasingly impenetrable language to an increasingly restricted audience' (McDonald 2003). Perhaps the gap results from the difficulty of translating theory into practice, leading some observers calling for more research into marketing implementation rather than marketing strategy. Practitioners are most eager to learn when confronted with change, and Relationship Marketing was a "big new idea" of the 1990s which businesses were eager to learn more about. A reason for much of practitioners' (and academics') current questioning of Relationship Marketing may stem from the shallowness of much early research which inadequately explored the sociological and psychological contexts of relationships, A challenge for Relationship Marketing is to develop multi-disciplinary insights into relationships which can be translated into operational relevance to businesses.

DO RELATIONSHIPS BELONG TO A UNIQUE CONCEPTUAL DOMAIN?

The academic discussion of Relationship Marketing has too often been polemic by regarding Relationship Marketing and transaction marketing as mutually exclusive domains. More recent thinking has come to see transaction marketing and Relationship Marketing as interdependent, with repeated transactions contributing, behaviorally and attitudinally, to relationship development. Ehrenberg (2000) has provided some new insights to the transaction-relationship dichotomy by suggesting that loyalty to a brand can develop instantly. In one study, new brands' average purchase frequency at launch was seen to be already normal, i.e., at the same level as a year or two later and at a level similar to established competitive brands. Traditional transaction marketing techniques of introductory discounts and point of sale promotion appeared to have successfully developed a relationship between customers and the products they bought (Ehrenberg, and Goodhardt, 2000). In another study of a financial services organization, the bank under investigation was not seen to engage in effective transaction or relationship planning or implementation but rather the managerial and organizational focus was on sales and promotion. The terms "transaction" and "relationship" did not seem to appear in managers' vocabulary (Walsh, Gilmore and Carson 2004).

In their paper, Pels and Saren note a distinction between the US based approach to relationships, which are seen as being an intensification of transactional marketing approaches, while from a European perspective, relationships derive from a series of transaction episodes. More recently, a third position–the Contemporary Marketing Practice–CMP–approach has emerged which argues that both paradigms can coexist. Pels and Saren argue that the transactional approach and the relational approach are strongly influenced by two different underlying worldviews, with different assumptions, understandings and philosophical bases. Our own epistemological framework influences the type of relationships that we see.

The recent conceptualization by Vargo and Lusch (2004) of a "service dominant" logic has implications for the domain of Relationship Marketing. Vargo and Lusch have argued for the pre-eminence of an ongoing service perspective, by means of ongoing interaction with a product and the people who sold it. In their conceptualization of economics systems, services form a focal point for value creation, and manufactured goods merely support the central value created by a service orientation. Could this service dominant logic be extended one stage further by arguing that all economic activity flows from relationships? In much the same way as service elements comprise an important element of even the most tangible manufactured goods, relationships are present in the manufacture and distribution of most products.

Growing interest in Mass Customization has focused on the role of relationships. Proponents of mass customization point to the growing importance of applying an experiential perspective of consumer behavior, implying that all companies need to understand the complex subjectivity involved in consumption, and should seek to develop unique formulations of products which satisfy each individual's needs (Addis and Holbrook, 2001). For many products, there has been the tendency to shift from mass marketing of a homogenous product to anonymous buyers towards customization of product to meet the needs of known individuals whose needs have become apparent through some form of dialogue based relationship.

In their paper, Varey and Ballantyne focus on dialogue as a defining characteristic of buyer-seller relationships. They challenge Relationship Marketing's hidden monological assumptions, and position dialogical interaction at the heart of Relationship Marketing. They draw the conclusion that dialogue is not so much a method of communication but an orientation to a form of relationship. The application of interpersonal communication theory is seen as useful for the process of positioning Relationship Marketing as an essentially social phenomenon. A dialogically induced shift in Relationship Marketing theory and practice would require some rethinking of marketing's reliance on communication at a long distance through mass communication channels to a homogenous audience. The evident failure of many attempts at customer relationship management may be based on a flawed model of dialogue between buyer and seller, which in reality has often been a one-way flow of fairly homogenous messages. In his paper, Henneberg notes that the "soft" aspects of customer relationship management are the ones which typically fail, and these failures often focus on inappropriate configuration of dialogue between the buyer and seller, in an environment which is essentially systems driven.

Harwood returns to the subject of dialogue in the context of negotiation, and in a study based on 12 negotiations concerning the strategic development of relationships, she finds distinct patterns of verbal behavior at different stages of relational development. it is noted that the quality of interaction is a controllable determinant in satisfying customers, and it is suggested that up to two-thirds of information and operational knowledge derives from informal face-to-face interactions.

RELATIONSHIP MARKETING AND PROFITABILITY

Relationship Marketing strategies have often been justified as a means of improving a company's financial performance, and Reichheld's early paper on the effects on profits of increased customer retention has frequently been cited as a justification for a switch from transaction to Relationship Marketing (Reichheld 1996). There have been numerous subsequent attempts to demonstrate the financial effects on a company's profitability of ongoing buyer-seller relationships (e.g., Reinartz, and Kumar, 2003; Ahmad and Buttle, 2001).

Relationship Marketing remains challenged by evidence that customers who are satisfied with their relationship may nevertheless not return to a company (Brady and Cronin, 2001; Gerpott et al., 2001). A problem with much academic research into Relationship Marketing is that satisfaction and quality have been correlated with behavioral intention rather than actual behavior. However, the dangers of predicting actual behavior on the basis of intention has been noted (e.g., Newberry, Klemz, and Boshoff 2003). In the light of increasing levels of competition in most services markets, behavioral intention based on loyalty generated through good service can easily be broken. This has been attributed to a number of factors, including: greater choice and information available to customers; the "commoditization" of many categories of services, and increased levels of competition.

Numerous scholars have sought to define and measure relationship quality, either as a conceptual entity in itself or as a component of service quality more generally. In one study, relationship quality was defined as a higher-order construct of cooperation, adaptation, and atmosphere, and was shown to have a positive impact on service quality (Ka-shing and Ennew, 2004). However, the link between relationship quality and profitability is not clear. This is partly because the link between quality and profitability has increasingly been questioned. While many studies have found that better service providers have a significantly higher return on equity than poorer providers (e.g., Bates, Bates and Johnston 2003), more recent attention has turned to "return on investment" rather than "total quality management" as an objective for profit maximization (Barnes Fox, and Morris, 2004). In a study by Cronin and Taylor (1992) service quality did not appear to have a significant positive effect on intentions to purchase again. Passikoff (1997) cites a Juran Institute study which indicated that less than a third of top managers of US' largest corporations believed that their customer satisfaction programs yielded any economic benefit.

It is also questionable whether some characteristics of a relationship generate satisfaction in customers while others generate dissatisfaction (Galloway, 1999). It has not been clearly demonstrated whether improvement in one element will generate satisfaction, but its absence, or reduction will not generate dissatisfaction. Conversely the failure to achieve a standard in another element may generate dissatisfaction in the customer, though its presence will not necessarily generate satisfaction and repeat purchase.

The published empirical evidence on returns from Relationship Marketing has tended to be short term and focused on narrowly defined database activity, rather than firms' investments in the total brand relationship (Reinartz, and Kumar 2003). The apparent paradox remains of many service organizations who undertake little Relationship Marketing activity, but command high levels of profitable loyalty. As an example, the greatest growth in the airline sector has been amongst no frills "budget" airlines who have eschewed relationship based loyalty programs and high levels of customer service in return for very low fares as a point of difference with established "full-service" airlines. It has been reported that as a sector, the rate of return on no-frills airlines is higher than for full-service airlines (Airline news 2004).

Henneberg, in his paper, notes that only 20 percent of US financial institutions that have introduced customer relationship management increased their profitability as a result and this view of CRM as a generally unsuccessful strategy is shared by many consumers.

The pursuit of Relationship Marketing metrics is quite timely, but again, a diversity of approaches can be noted. CRM systems typically generate a lot of data which can be used inductively to build models of consumer behavior, or deductively to test assumptions and theories. Complex statistical models must be used in conjunction with more qualitative approaches if a full understanding of consumers' relationships with a company are to be gained. As an example, the retailer Tesco is widely reported to have used it us extensive database, which combines sales data and loyalty program data, to identify a correlation in its stores between sales of beer and sales of nappies (diapers). Cross-sectional data and longitudinal data gave a measure of one aspect of its customers' relationship with the company, but the data alone offered no explanation of causation. For this, further qualitative research was required. Through qualitative research, the company eventually found that the male in a household was offering to do a good turn by going to the store to buy diapers, when in reality, he saw this as an excuse and an opportunity to get out of the house to buy beer. But should it have taken such an extensive program of data collection and analysis to gain this knowledge? The owner of the typical Irish pub has known for a long time that consumers often need an excuse to visit the pub, hence the appearance of post offices and grocery stores that are incorporated into the pub. The Irish pub owner has used its relationship with customers and a sound understanding of consumer behavior to configure their product offer in a way that Tesco could only achieve with the help of a huge database. The challenge of Relationship Marketing is to recreate in large organizations the informed and flexible relationships which have been at the heart of many small businesses' practices.

REFERENCES

Addis, Michela; Holbrook, Morris B (2001), On the conceptual link between mass customization and experiential consumption: An explosion of subjectivity, *Journal of Consumer Behavior*, Vol. 1 (1), pp. 50-66.

Ahmad, R., Buttle, F. (2001), "Retaining business customers through adaptation and bonding," *Journal of Business and Industrial Marketing*, Vol. 16, (7), pp. 553-573.

Airline News (2004), Slump in US airlines' profits, http://news.airwise.com/story/view/11152469.html

Bates, K.; Bates, H. and Johnston, R. (2003) Linking service to profit: the business case for service excellence International, *Journal of Service Industry Management*, 14 (2), pp. 173–183.

Barnes, Bradley R.; Fox, Martin T.; Morris, D. S, (2004), Exploring the linkage between internal marketing, relationship marketing and service quality, *Total Quality Management & Business Excellence*, Jul/Aug 2004, Vol. 15 (5/6), pp. 593-601.

Brady, M.K., Cronin, J.J., 2001, "Some new thoughts on conceptualizing perceived service quality: a hierarchical approach," *Journal of Marketing*, 65, pp. 34-49.

Burton, Dawn (2001), Critical marketing theory: the blueprint, *European Journal of Marketing, Volume* 35 (5/6), pp. 722-743.

Christopher, M., Payne, A. and Ballantyne, D., (1991), "Relationship Marketing," Butterworth-Heinemann.

Coviello, N.E., Brodie, R.J and Munro, H.J. (1997), "Understanding contemporary marketing: development of a classification scheme," *Journal of Marketing Management*, Vol.13, pp. 501-52.

Cronin J J and S A Taylor, 1992: Measuring Service Quality: A Re-examination and Extension, *Journal of Marketing*, Vol. 56 (July), 55-68.

Ehrenberg, Andrew and Goodhardt, Gerald, 2000, New Brands: Near-Instant Loyalty, *Journal of Marketing Management*, Jul 2000, Vol. 16 (6), pp. 607-617.

Ehrensal, K.N., 1999, "*Critical management studies and the American business school culture: or, how not to get tenure in one easy publication,*" paper presented at the Critical Management Studies Conference, Manchester School of Management, UMIST, Manchester.

Galloway, L. 1999, Hysteresis: A model of consumer behaviour? *Managing Service Quality*, Vol 9 (5), pp. 360-370.

Gerpott, T., Rams, W.; Schindler, A, (2001) "Customer Retention, loyalty, and satisfaction in the German mobile cellular telecommunications market," *Telecommunications Policy, 25* pp. 249-269.

Gladwell, M. (2000), The Tipping Point: *How Little Things Can Make a Big Difference*, New York, Little Brown and Co.

Gummeson, E. (1987), "The new marketing–developing long-term interactive relationships," *Long Range Planning, Vol. 20, pp. 10-20.*

Ka-shing Woo; Ennew, Christine F (2004), Business-to-business relationship quality, European Journal of *Marketing*, Vol. 38 (9/10), pp. 1252-1271.

McDonald, M., (2003), "Marketing died in the last decade," *Interactive Marketing*, Vol. 5 (2), pp. 144-159.

Newberry, C.RF., Klemz, B.R. and Boshoff, C. (2003), Managerial implications of predicting purchase behavior from purchase intentions: a retail patronage case study, *Journal of Services Marketing*, Vol. 17 (6), pp. 609-20.

Passikoff, R. (1997), The limits of customer satisfaction, *Brandweek*, Vol. 38, No. 9, p. 17.

Reichheld, F. (1996), *The loyalty Effect*. Cambridge MA: Harvard Business School Press.

Reinartz, Werner and Kumar, V. (2003), The Impact of Customer Relationship Characteristics on Profitable Lifetime Duration, *Journal of Marketing*. Vol 67(1), pp. 77- 99.

Vargo, S L. and Lusch.R.F. (2004), Evolving to a New Dominant Logic for Marketing. *Journal of Marketing*, Volume 68 (1), pp. 1-17.

Walsh, Susan; Gilmore, Audrey; Carson, David (2004), Managing and implementing simultaneous transaction and relationship marketing, *International Journal of Bank Marketing*, 2004, Vol. 22 (7), pp. 468-473.

Wensley, R., 1999, "Commentary," in Brownlie, D., Saren, M., Wensley, R., Whittington, R., *Rethinking Marketing*, Sage, London.

Relationship Marketing and the Challenge of Dialogical Interaction

Richard J. Varey

Waikato Management School, University of Waikato, New Zealand

David Ballantyne

University of Otago School of Business, New Zealand

SUMMARY. Our aim in this article is to challenge relationship marketing's hidden monological assumptions, and as a redress, position dialogical interaction at its core. First, we reflect on the common sense of 'marketing communication'. Next, we clarify the concept of 'dialogue'. We then comment on the concept of dialogue in markets, building on Karl Popper's idea of an open society, followed by scrutiny of general marketing practice to show that such dialogue is absent. We then consider the potential for marketing to be dialogical in nature. To do this we will make a necessary distinction between *informational* interaction, *communicational* interaction, and *dialogical* interaction. Finally, we draw

Richard J. Varey, PhD, is Professor of Marketing, and Chair, Department of Marketing and International Management, Waikato Management School, University of Waikato, New Zealand (E-mail: rvarey@mngt.waikato.ac.nz).

David Ballantyne, PhD, is Associate Professor, University of Otago School of Business, Dunedin, New Zealand (E-mail: ballantyne.david@bigpond.com).

[Haworth co-indexing entry note]: "Relationship Marketing and the Challenge of Dialogical Interaction." Varey, Richard J., and David Ballantyne. Co-published simultaneously in *Journal of Relationship Marketing* (Best Business Books, an imprint of The Haworth Press, Inc.) Vol. 4, No. 3/4, 2005, pp. 11-28; and: *The Future of Relationship Marketing* (ed: David Bejou, and Adrian Palmer) Best Business Books, an imprint of The Haworth Press, Inc., 2005, pp. 11-28. Single or multiple copies of this article are available for a fee from The Haworth Document Delivery Service [1-800-HAWORTH, 9:00 a.m. - 5:00 p.m. (EST). E-mail address: docdelivery@haworthpress.com].

the conclusion that dialogue is not so much a method of communication but an orientation to it, and consider some implications for marketing theory and practice. *[Article copies available for a fee from The Haworth Document Delivery Service: 1-800-HAWORTH. E-mail address: <docdelivery@haworthpress.com> Website: <http://www.HaworthPress.com>* © *2005 by The Haworth Press, Inc. All rights reserved.]*

KEYWORDS. Interaction, communication, dialogue

INTRODUCTION

Marketing dialogue is emerging as a topic for discussion in articles and books, and at conferences and lectures. A basic search of the World Wide Web (using the Google.com search engine) in the Spring of 2004 located several hundred documents containing the term "marketing dialogue". Also, dialogue is the theme of a special issue on relationship marketing in the *Journal of Business and Industrial Marketing* (Ballantyne, 2004a). At the pedagogical level, a new undergraduate text in marketing with a 'value' orientation (Gabbott, 2003) includes a chapter titled 'Communicating through Interaction and Dialogue'. This dialogical *turn* in marketing communication seems long overdue, and further research activity can be anticipated. No common understanding is prevalent at this stage.

Several related observations are worthwhile at the outset. First, the dominant form of modern marketing practice operates as a one-way message making system grounded in mass communication theory (DeLozier, 1976). Second, commonplace thinking accepts as normal the decoupling of interaction and communication (Varey, 2002b). Third, the notion of authentic dialogue fits well with the re-ascendant notion of relationships in marketing. On the other hand, in everyday use the term *dialogue* is unreflectively taken to mean an extended conversation among two or more people. By way of contrast, our notion of dialogue embodies a pre-industrial perspective on human interaction, set in the context of post-industrial marketing. In other words, confusion and opportunity abound.

In this article, we will argue that dialogical communication among marketing stakeholders is necessary for an enterprise to be an innovative social and economic contributor. First, we will reflect on the common sense of 'marketing communication' as it is understood today.

Next, we clarify and present our concept of dialogue. We then comment on the concept of dialogue in markets, building on Karl Popper's idea of an open society, followed by scrutiny of general marketing practice to show that such dialogue is absent. We then consider the potential for marketing to be dialogical in nature. To do this we will make a necessary distinction between *informational* interaction, *communicational* interaction, and *dialogical* interaction. Finally, we draw the conclusion that dialogue is not so much a method of communication but an orientation to it, and consider the implications for relationship marketing theory and practice.

THE COMMON SENSE OF MARKETING COMMUNICATION

Marketing communication is the underlying process through which marketing activity and resources are converted into economic outcomes. However, if we emphasize economic outcomes, without due regard for their enabling processes, we can miss the obvious point that marketing is grounded in strategic (purposeful) social interaction (Varey, 2002a).

According to Deetz (1995), the intent of marketing management activity is to control the market (constituted by supply chains and mass communication) so as to make sales in competition with other sellers. Thus managers tend to strive to control their own destiny and that of their firm, rather than anticipate and respond to service needs (i.e., provision of supportive problem-solving products). Ethical questions are subsumed in the assumed appropriateness of self-interested profit maximization. With efficient delivery systems and performance and the presumption of free market choice (people acting as consumers), ethical questions seldom need be asked. This control-driven, self-interest finds expression in the monological (or one-way) mode of marketing communication that is dominant today. Managers and firms gain short-run advantage from this, but it is unclear how societies or indeed any of a firm's constituent stakeholders benefit in the long run.

The universally pervasive linear transmissive model of communication (originated as a model of 'information' by Shannon and Weaver, 1949) gives primacy to the role of 'sender' as the dominant agent. This is because the agent that controls the mechanisms to enable the flow of information also controls the communicative act/event with the chosen 'receiver'[1] While this is a plausible if somewhat mechanistic explanation for single one-way messages, it misrepresents the spontaneous nature of continuing interaction and collaboration implied in voluntary marketing exchange. Yet in spite of its limitations, the transmissive model remains the dominant communication logic in marketing texts and in use, notwithstanding attempts to introduce more interactive perspectives over the last decade, as embodied in direct marketing, and Integrated Marketing Communication (IMC) (see for example, Dauer, 1992; Grönroos and Lindberg-Repo, 1998).

What is needed, in our view, is an escape route from the limiting, monological communication model that *scientises* all explanation, prediction and design for marketing interaction. There are signs of such developments. First, Duncan and Moriarty (1997) have proposed using IMC to sustain stakeholder relationships and profitably. Second, and more recently, Lindberg-Repo and Gronroos (2004) proposed a communication framework to show time-related and dynamical aspects of communicative interaction, based on the assumption that the communication process between a buyer and seller evolves towards dialogue through three specific *communicative acts*, or modalities. These modes (in common order of progression) are: planned communications, contact creation, and connectedness. Together, they can generate mutual value and strengthen relationships over time. Third, the potential for using a variety of forms of communication, from monologue to dialogue, has been presented in a *marketing communication matrix* by Ballantyne (2004b). This matrix includes one-way messages from the focal firm directed 'to' or 'for' its customers and other parties, where 'to' represents the basic offering, and 'for' represents a more value added and targeted format. As well, there is recognition of two-way communication 'with' customers and other parties; and also dialogical interaction 'between' the focal firm and its customers and other parties (see Figure 1).

In creating a nexus between dialogical interaction and relationship marketing, one problem is that common use of the term can often mean no more than a conversational approach to stimulating a hoped-for purchase and/or use-of-product response.[2] We need to return to an earlier *common sense* notion of what it once meant to be dialogical in communication. The application of interpersonal communication theory (Cherry, 1978; Hovland et al., 1953; Schramm, 1963; Watzlawick et al., 1967) is a useful start to regaining the sense of marketing as a social phenomenon—as implied by 'relationship' marketing, but also by the concept 'marketing' itself. This would require recognition of markets as comprising sellers *and* buyers, all of whom are *social actors* who interact to achieve economic outcomes. Furthermore, a dialogically induced shift in marketing theory and practice would require some rethinking of mar-

FIGURE 1. Marketing Communication Matrix

ONE-WAY	Communication 'to'	Communication 'for'	
The conventional managerial approaches, giving prominence to the planning and crafting of persuasive informational messages	Planned persuasive messages aimed at securing brand awareness and loyalty	Planned persuasive messages but with augmented offerings for targeted markets	
(Many messages will remain unopened, unseen and unheard)	e.g., Communicating the 'unique selling proposition' to the mass market in concrete and symbolic terms	e.g., Communicating targeted customer life cycle products; product or service guarantees; loyalty programs	
TWO-WAY		Communication 'with'	Communication 'between'
Communicative interaction, both formal and informal, which may be prompted by planned messages 'to' or 'for' customers, as above		Integrated mix of planned messages and interactively shared knowledge	Dialogue between participants based on trust, learning and adaptation, with co-created outcomes
(This includes more spontaneous and dialogical approaches between participants that give prominence to listening and learning)		e.g., Face to face encounters e.g., Direct (data-base) marketing e.g., Call centers e.g., Interactive B2B internet portals.	e.g., Key account liaison between two or more firms e.g., Expansion of communities of common interest, often Internet based e.g., Teamwork between staff project groups within one firm, or between firms

| **Mass markets** | **Portfolio/ Mass-customized** | **Networks** |

← ── →

Source: Ballantyne (2004b)

keting's reliance on the efficacy of communicating at long distance through mediators to a homogenous 'mass'. In fact, this kind of communication–the act of *uttering*–is not really communication at all but simply message making. As put by Luhmann (2000, p. 4):

> ... communication only comes about when someone watches, listens, reads–and understands to the extent that further communication could follow on. The mere act of uttering does not constitute communication.

On this basis, much so called 'marketing communication' comprises unopened messages, unrequited messages, and deliberate message avoidance on the part of the target receiver. For Luhmann, an eminent social philosopher, the venue for most marketing utterances (whether spoken and written) is the mass media. In this the advertiser seeks to manipulate and works insincerely, assuming that this behavior is taken for granted by observers. Yet, while advertising may declare its motives, it refines and often conceals its methods. The intention is to control purchase and consumption by reminding people that there is something to buy and that a particular name or product deserves special attention. Consumers recognize that what they see is advertising, but not how they are influenced. According to Luhmann (2000), consumers believe that they freely choose whenever they decide that they want something.

In Luhmann's analysis (2000), mass media operators all but rule out interaction between message senders and receivers through the interposition of media technology. As has been discussed, the marketer-advertiser communication model is strategic and linear–a *copy/duplicate* theory of meaning.

If Luhmann is correct, this kind of marketing communication does not begin to explain how we generate and circulate information, co-create meaning, or achieve flashes of inspired, co-created value.

ON DIALOGUE

Dialogue in marketing has been defined as an interactive process of learning together (Ballantyne, 2004b). Derived from the Greek *dialegesthai*, the original meaning was to think and speak about something in such as way that the thing the speakers were talking about was recognized as different, and in talking together, the speakers were able to move toward a new intellectual understanding. Dialogue holds the promise of revealing something new, and implies a developmental shift in the relationship between the parties involved. Dialogue is also a useful communicative approach to knowledge development within and between organizations. A dialogical approach may well allow participants to disagree on what those new knowledge positions ought to be. It follows that dialogue cannot be reduced to one person's activity alone, or reduced to one person's perspective alone–it is inherently relational. Clearly, the transmissive model of communicating does not hold for dialogue, since the intention in engaging in communicative interaction is not unidirectional, self-serving control and accomplishment. On the contrary, the purpose of dialogue, by our reasoning, is open ended, discovery oriented, mutually achievable and value creating.

The first problem in using the term *dialogical* is linguistic and semantic. Much so-called dialogue is no more than two-way combative (dialectical) monologues, or at best, message making with feedback–the hoped-for prize is acceptance of one party's asserted claims in support of an ideological or commercial preference relating exclusively to self-interest. However, in dialogue, participants speak and act *between* each other, not *to* each other. While the outcomes are economic there is a social purpose fulfilled so long as no party is treated as a means to an exclusively private end. This ethical dialogical resolve can best be experienced through interactions built on trust.

ON MARKETS

George Soros' (2000) adaptation of Karl Popper's concept of an *open society* (Popper, 1945) makes the point that traditional markets (as places for the exchange of goods and mediated by money) are entirely suitable for the pursuit of private interest but not well suited at all to the pursuit of common interest.[3] It has been said that the transition from oral communicative traditions to writing has *decoupled* interaction from communication; and further, the transition from writing to electronic media has decoupled communication from information (Kittler, 1996). Certainly, dialogue as we have defined it does not seem to serve the short term interests of powerful sellers, and there is the added confusion that some forms of marketing dialogue are not dialogues at all. Thus an interesting question is whether dialogue can occur when communication is mediated by mass media? Are we, in speaking of marketing dialogue, aspiring to a mechanism that cannot operate in markets?

An open society, according to Popper (1945), is an association of free individuals respecting one another's rights within a framework of law. The open society is open to improvement, whereas the closed society denies its own imperfections even as the world around it changes. Nevertheless, according to Popper, an open society is always threatened by the unbridled pursuit of self-interest. Also, any ideology that makes claims of possessing ultimate truth and seeks to impose that truth by compulsion and other repressive measures is an obstacle to maintaining an open society, as minority self-interest regulates and constrains the greater good.[4]

Dialogue may be a necessary basis for the authentic pursuit of innovation and creativity in markets, that is, for changing markets and societal behaviors in a broader sense. Of course a *reframed* marketing philosophy would be necessary in parallel to such changes, making a departure from the biased/manipulative/mendacious disciplining in pursuit of short term economic exchange outcomes. This would mean 'breaking free' from the dominant logic of marketing, and indeed informational interaction, as has been discussed.

Marketing seen as a social process with economic outcomes grounded in social networks of dialogical interaction could build on a range of communicative actions with dialogue at its centre. Of course, marketing, in its modern principles and in practices, has not been seen as a dialogical social activity. Yet, the central concept of marketing is *exchange*. Is not exchange a reciprocal event? What detracts from the fluidity of the marketing concept is the almost universal presupposition of unidirectional, goal-seeking behavior–where marketing is seen to be successful at the point that the 'targeted' object (buyer) yields to the persuasion of the seller. Thus, marketing has become a way of living life for a profit of restricted value.

DIALOGUE IN MARKETS

Marketing behavior (that is, the activity that brings about buying and selling) can be analyzed in terms of its patterns of interaction, specifically in preparing for exchange, and interaction during that exchange. The former is concerned with when to interact, and why. The latter is concerned with the way that interaction is conducted and resolved.

A more radical relationship-oriented way of thinking about dialogue in markets is now proposed. To begin, consider the extent to which typical market interactions are, or can be, dialogical in nature and purpose. Some examples of common marketing practices that violate or deny the essence of dialogical relating are summarized in Table 1, following Johannesen's (1971) characterization of dialogical relating (shown in the left hand column).

These characteristics suggest to us that what is popularly termed 'relationship marketing' is not dialogical but uses the notion of *relating* falsely to suggest committed and highly responsive trading. Indeed, the terms 'relationship' and 'dialogue' are often applied by suppliers when no genuine relationship is intended or sought (see, for example, McKenna, 1991). For example, many customers experience irritation at data base-driven, automated machine-person encounters in making everyday telephone enquiries. Likewise, large-scale call center automation located at distance from customers serves productivity well, leaving many unre-

TABLE 1. Characteristics of Dialogical Relationship Orientation and Monological Marketing Orientation–Compared

DIALOGICAL–LEARNING ORIENTATION	MONOLOGICAL–INFORMING ORIENTATION
Mutual openness: Sense of responsibility, mutuality, honesty, communion	*Strategies for communication efficiency that place large-scale technical systems as an interface between people, preventing personal interaction*
Non-manipulative: Influence without manipulative intent (e.g., propaganda and deception); one's beliefs not forced on others	*Exaggerated claims, unrealistic promises, manipulative advertising messages, corporate mendacity*
Recognition of uniqueness: Individuality of the other is acknowledged, with equal rights and respect	*Crude segmentation, people characterized as consumers, and trading relationships rendered into numbers by 'data mining' in 'data warehouses.'*
Mutual confirmation: Confirmation and acceptance of the other, but not as an observer	*Mass market advertising, direct mail, junk mail–all forms of impersonal 'message' sending*
Turning toward: Meeting in unreserved expression and without desire for creating appearances	*Image-making, narcissist behavior*
Non-evaluative: Attempts to see the other's point-of-view–heeding, affirming and confirming	*Refusal to accept or ignorance of customer complaints–objectifying 'buyers'*

Source: Based on Johannesen, 1971

solved challenges for relationship marketing. This is because the mechanistic system-orientated way of producing and delivering marketing value (Ritzer & Stillman, 2001) is premised on a particular set of beliefs about modes of communication within an instrumentally rational mindset. This is blatantly obvious in Customer Relationship Management (CRM) where the information systems used are a convergence of 'expert' service systems and 'relationally' structured information technologies. Human relationships and human thinking processes have been de-centered in this kind of relationship marketing logic.

Barnes (2001) has argued that most marketing relationships are not genuine human relationships–they don't take into account each other's point of view, especially in considering respective expectations of the relationship. The inherent emotional and social basis for the relationship is unrecognized or ignored. Instead the focus is on the seller's perspective, repeat purchases, frequency of contacts, duration of dealings or similar behaviors, as if these were authentic manifestations of 'loyalty'. Similarly, in some discussions of Customer Relationship Management (CRM), the relationship is espoused *as if* social in nature, when every indication is that the relationship in action is really no more than the capture and circulation of information about the customer. Clearly, there is a fundamental tension in the impact of technology on relationships within organizations and markets (Zuboff, 1988).

Yet the value-creating boundaries are where ethical market actors want them. For example, in researching B2B markets, Håkansson and Johanson (1992), avoided the excesses of reductionism by explaining networks of business relationships as a three way interdependency between *actor bonds*, and *resource ties*, and *activity links*. Indeed, all marketing can be understood as interaction within networks of relationships (Gummesson, 1999). And if we see marketing exchange as an open ended process, it follows that interactions are the enactment of that process (Ballantyne, 2004b). Our perspective is that traditional marketing has undervalued the idea of buyer-seller interaction because it leads to an open ended co-creation of value that is not exclusively controlled by the seller.

CAN MARKETING BE DIALOGIC?

Buber, in his theological/philosophical writings, (1966) indicates that engaging in dialogue with another person does not mean that one party might not try to influence the other. The key point here is that in aiming to influence in dialogue, we must present our position in a non-coercive, non-manipulative manner, one that respects the free choice and individuality of the other. As Buber put it (1966, p. 112):

> The desire to influence the other then does not mean the effort to change the other, to inject one's own 'rightness' into him; but it means the effort to let that which is recognized as right, as just, as true . . . through one's influence take seed and grow in the form suited to individuation.

Of course the principle of such ethical communication could be applied to all interpersonal interactions, and those of small group, public address, and mass communication. In Buber's sense of the dialogue, there is no place for falsification or attempted manipulation in what is discussed or how the discussion proceeds. Critically, the locus of power lies between the participants. This dialogical sharing of control requires mutual trust. It should not surprise us that the term 'communication' derives from '*munia*,' meaning the mutual help, exchange, and interaction of those *belonging* to the same community (of which the *market* is a social construction). According to Johannesen (1971, p. 375), participants in dialogue

> . . . *aid each other in making responsible decisions regardless of whether the decision be favorable or unfavorable to the particular view presented.*

The ethical principles of marketing communication are often taken for granted among marketing academics and practitioners. However, if it is accepted that monologue is the antithesis of dialogue, then Gaw and Makay (1975) offer a revealing check list of the aims and concerns of monological communicators:

- primary concern for power over the other
- primary concern with persuasion for profit, regardless of whether or not ends justify means
- primary concern with personal prestige and status
- primary concern with shaping the other's image regardless of the other's unique self
- primary concern with self-aggrandizement

Could marketing communication be dialogic, more often? Following Buber (1966) the answer is a qualified yes, when marketing interactions are characterized by:

- mutuality, honesty, a non-manipulative approach
- absence of imposing beliefs on the other
- recognition of uniqueness
- mutual confirmation
- respectfully giving attention to the other
- non-evaluative, attempting to see your partner's point-of-view even when opposed to yours

With these critical imperatives before us as a basis for judgment, only rarely could traditional marketing qualify as dialogical. While marketing's embedded motives remain control and profit maximization, it becomes difficult to imagine how marketing interaction could also be driven by a genuine concern for people. Yet these positions are not irreconcilable. Such reconciliation requires a longer-term view and a learning perspective in which dialogue might find a place. Any charge of naive altruistic intent can be addressed rationally on the basis that respect for the needs of the other is a prerequisite for our own need fulfillment.

In co-creating value through dialogue and learning, the reciprocal success benchmark becomes "If it is better for us, then it becomes better for me". This involves a shift in strategic perspective to a recognize a broader view of *stakeholder interests*, which in turn requires a shifting of mental models to accommodate the idea of a 'market' as a socially constructed *network* of relationships where interactions have economic consequences. For example, the 'six markets' relationship model proposed by Christopher et al. (2002) specifically brings various stakeholder groups and their interests into marketing planning cycles. Other approaches to classifying a firm's stakeholders include those of Kotler (1992), Morgan and Hunt (1994) and Gummesson (1994).

CONCLUSIONS

We have argued that the potential to extend marketing interaction to the dialogical level is always available. This is especially so in service industries, B2B markets and not-for-profits, as well as in new product development and internal marketing projects. However, we see widespread inconsistency in what is espoused concerning relationships, interaction, and dialogue. In particular, mass media message making and technologically enabled marketing interaction in relationship marketing have become ubiquitous (see for example, Fournier et al., 1998). The ultimate distillation of the relationships ideal is when Customer Relationship Management (CRM) is practiced as a technology enabled information capturing and circulating system, where the only 'relationships' of note are between data.

We conceive of marketing, especially relationship marketing, as grounded in interaction in potentially three ways. First as informational, second, as communicational, and third, as dialogical (see Table 2). The *informational mode* includes all message-making which has the useful intention to inform. The more manipulative practices of 'transactional marketing' and much of what currently passes as CRM are extreme versions of this. Next, much of marketing's current relationship oriented aspirations are grounded in the *communicational* mode, where listening

TABLE 2. A Classification of Interaction Modes

Mode of interaction	Underlying political and decision practices	Source of value	Form of market system co-ordination
Informational: persuasive message making	Controlling and dominating	Supplied by persuasive *selling* of the benefits	Hierarchy
Communicational: informing and listening	Integrated communicative interaction and stakeholder equity	Negotiated value co-produced through promise-making and promise-keeping	Interactive
Dialogical: learning together	Finding a voice in co-determination	Emergent value co-created in *learning*	Network

and informing are the product of interaction, especially in services marketing, and B2B marketing. Finally, our view of the unrealised potential of marketing interaction is in the *dialogical* mode, as has been discussed. These categories are conceived of as *ideal types* following Weberian tradition. In other words, they are pure constructs and some category overlap is likely in practice. We do not claim that they are moral or ethical categories.

There are parallels in our three-part classification to Deetz's (1995) analysis, where he distinguishes between *informing* from *communicating* modes of interaction. However, our interest in *dialogical interaction* goes further, radically expanding the 'something for something' notion of marketing exchange. Dialogue as we have defined it brings opportunities for generating value in new ways, both within the firm and between firms, as *co-created solutions* for market and supply problems and opportunities. Furthermore, the particular circumstance of value creation means it is difficult for competitors to copy. In this way, unique *collaborative* advantage might be achieved through dialogue.

Clearly, dialogical interaction is a big step-up from informational interaction. The former is grounded in personal interaction and learning together, whereas the latter is associated with mass media message-making. More attention is given to the product (or people as objects) in informational interaction, and to people (as dialogical interacts) in dialogical interaction.

The problem with marketing communication is not a *communication problem* as such but a problem of myopia, misconception and restricted communicative choices. What is being overlooked in marketing communication is the power and variety of interaction in all its forms. Marketing communication has been locked into a way of thinking that sees message making as *the* dominant mode. Working on the false notion that a message can possess a fixed meaning, marketing has focused attention and resources on the means of coding these messages and regulating their transmission. This is done for the purpose of trying to change other peoples' choices. This is how it has been in the past, and this is what has been carried forward relatively unchallenged to the present time.

Our test for dialogical authenticity is whether interaction brings opportunities for learning together. Dialogue in marketing is not so much a method of communication but an *orientation* to it. A dialogical orientation in marketing takes message making to be merely an initiator or first step towards co-producing meaning, knowledge, and value. For example, Grönroos (2000, p. 280), has provided a cyclical representation of this process where the co-determination of value between any buyer and seller can be open ended and continuing). We would add that the co-determination of value can be open ended and continuing within a network of buyers and sellers, or within a network of customers (word-of-mouth), or within an internal network of employees (as communities with a common interest).

Of course there are constraints to increasing the spiral of communicative reciprocity, which have to be acknowledged as well. There is always potential for the frustration of intentions between buyer and seller, and indeed other stakeholders. There is the possibility of a mismatch of expectations. Or one party may attempt to control the interaction by establishing a purely *informational* engagement. Alternatively, one party may attempt to interact in *dialogical* mode, but is met by an informational response. And perhaps some of the time the parties involved will understand each other quite well but just don't want to agree!

IMPLICATIONS FOR PRACTICE

First, dialogue aims at developing an *understanding* of each participant's point of view and interaction sets up suitable conditions for listening and learning together. Dialogue in marketing is much more than alternating monologues, and covers the joint investigation of needs, wants, desires, problems, issues, and decisions to be made. To achieve this grand aspiration, at least some of the time, we have to do better than attending to service quality issues and identifying mechanistic CRM mediated contact opportunities as 'touch points'. Instead, we suggest that marketers might experimentally and selectively engage in dialogical inquiry (listening and learning) and so become more reflective of the consequences of past actions. Dialogical interaction is not the alternate propounding of opinions with the intent of winning over any argument offered by the other party–dialogical outcomes go beyond one's own understanding and so finding creative solutions to previously intractable problems is quite possible.

Second, dialogue creatively *disrupts* the taken-for-granted and unspoken assumptions that restrict commitment and satisfaction to the ordinary. Dialogue is not simply a two-way dissemination of information for decision-making and action. Any cognitive dissonance induced by dialogue can be positive if there is mutual effort and trust. We conclude that not everyone is ready for dialogue but this can be tested in practice, interactively, and incrementally. Give or take some attempts at persuasion at the outset, and then some experience in mutual informing and listening, extraordinary dialogical exchanges can occur when the trust level is adequate to the anticipated risk involved.

Third, dialogue may lead to *common agreement* on any particular issue, or perhaps a variety of different interpretations will remain in play. It is quite possible to achieve understanding even if the parties agree to differ. Dialogical interaction means becoming more aware of routine but hidden thought patterns and assumptions held by ourselves and by others. In dialogue, an attempt is made to query your participants' assumptions and prejudices and likewise to confront your own, some of which are always really difficult to access (for a detailed examination of the nature of these basic assumptions, see Ballantyne, 2004b). We conclude that the mutual checking of assumptions is fundamental to learning together, and helpful in reaching more enlightened exchanges of mutual value.

Finally, just as there can be different kinds of marketing relationships and levels of depth, so it is in dialogue. The challenge for relationship marketing is in accepting dialogical interaction as a guiding ideal. Creative practical applications flow from that.

NOTES

1. The technical concept of 'information' first evident as recently as in Hartley's work (1928) avoids any reference to ideas or meaning, and thus to people.

2. One of the authors has recently seen a software product brochure that claims that the product "makes sure you ask the right people about the relevant issues at the right

time by engaging them in one-to-one interactive dialogues at key touch points in the relationship." What does this promise mean? What would a dialogue that is *not* interactive be like? Further, in a recent article by a leading US brand consultant, it is claimed that a "marketing dialogue between brands and consumers" is replacing "the one-way conversation" of advertising. How does a collection of signs and artefacts interact with a person such that dialogue is possible?

3. Muller, 2002, has traced the history of idea of the market in modern European thinking.

4. Managerialism as an ideology may be such an obstacle. It is beyond the scope of this paper to elaborate further, however, see Deetz (1992).

REFERENCES

Ballantyne, D. (2004a). "Pathways less traveled to value creation: interaction, dialogue and knowledge generation." *Journal of Business and Industrial Marketing*, 19(2), 97-98.

Ballantyne, D. (2004b). "Dialogue and its role in the development of relationship specific knowledge." *Journal of Business and Industrial Marketing*, 19(2), 114-123.

Barnes, J. G. (2001). *Secrets of Customer Relationship Management: It's All About How You Make Them Feel*. New York: McGraw-Hill.

Buber, M. in Glatzer, N. (ed.) (1966). *Buber: The Way of Response. Selections from his Writings*. New York: Schocken Books.

Cherry, C. (1978). *On Human Communication: A Review, A Survey, and a Criticism* (3rd Edition). Cambridge, MA: MIT Press.

Christopher, M., Payne, A. and Ballantyne, D. (2002). *Relationship Marketing: Creating Stakeholder Value* (2nd Edition). Oxford: Butterworth-Heinemann.

Dauer, J. (1992). "Interactive multiple communications architecture." Paper presented at the *2nd Annual Symposium on Integrated Marketing Communications*. IL, Northwestern University.

Deetz, S. A. (1992). *Democracy in an Age of Corporate Colonization: Developments in Communication and the Politics of Everyday Life*. Albany, NY: State University of New York.

Deetz, S. A. (1995). *Transforming Communication, Transforming Business: Building Responsive and Responsible Workplaces*. Creskill, NJ: Hampton Press.

DeLozier, M. W. (1976). *The Marketing Communications Process*. New York: McGraw-Hill.

Duncan, T., and Moriarty, S. (1997). *Driving Brand Value: Using Integrated Marketing to Manage Profitable Stakeholder Relationships*. New York: McGraw-Hill.

Fournier, S., Dobscha, S. and Mick, D. G. (1998). "Preventing the premature death of relationship marketing." *Harvard Business Review*, 96, Jan-Feb, 42-48.

Gaw, B. A. and Makay, J. J. (1975). *Personal and Interpersonal Communication: Dialogue with the Self and with Others*. Columbus, Ohio: Merrill Publishers.

Gabbott, M. (ed.) (2003). *An Introduction to Marketing: A Value Exchange Approach*. Harlow: Pearson Education.

Grönroos, C. (2000), *Service Management and Marketing: A Customer Relationship Management Approach*, Chichester: Wiley.

Grönroos, C. and Lindberg-Repo, K. (1998). "Integrated marketing communications: the communications aspect of relationship marketing." *Integrated Marketing Communications Research Journal*, 4(1), 3-11.

Gummesson, E. (1994). "Making relationship marketing operational." *International Journal of Service Industry Management*, 5(5), 5-20.

Gummesson, E. (1999). "Total relationship marketing: experimenting with a synthesis of research frontiers." *Australasian Marketing Journal*, 7(1), 72-85.

Håkansson, H. and Johanson, J. (1992). "A model of industrial networks." In Axelsson, B. and Easton, G. eds. *Industrial Networks–A New View of Reality*. London: Routledge.

Hartley, R. V. L. (1928). "Transmission of information." *The Bell System Technical Journal*. 7, 535-563.

Hovland, C. I., Janis, I. L. and Kelley, H. H. (1953). *Communication and Persuasion: Psychological Studies of Opinion Change*. New Haven, CT: Yale University Press.

Johannesen, R. L. (1971). "The Emerging concept of communication as dialogue." *The Quarterly Journal of Speech*, 57, December, 373-382.

Kittler, F. (1996). "The history of the communication media." *CTHEORY: The International Journal of Theory, Technology, and Culture* (On-line). *www.ctheory.net*

Kotler, P. (1992). "It's time for Total Marketing." *Business Week*, Advance Executive Brief, 2.

Lindberg-Repo, K. and Gronroos, C. (2004). "Conceptualising communications strategy from a relational perspective." *Industrial Marketing Management*, 33, 229-239.

Luhmann, N. (2000). *The Reality of the Mass Media*, Stanford, CA: Stanford University Press.

McKenna, R. (1991). *Relationship Marketing: Own the Market through Strategic Customer Relationships*. London: Century Business Books.

Morgan, R. M. and Hunt, S. D. (1994). "The commitment-trust theory of relationship marketing." *Journal of Marketing*, 58, July, 20-38.

Muller, J. Z. (2002). *The Mind and the Market: Capitalism in Modern European Thought*. New York: Alfred A Knopf.

Popper, K. R. (1945). *The Open Society and Its Enemies: The Spell of Plato*. London: Routledge/Kogan Page.

Ritzer, G. and Stillman, T. (2001). "From person-to-system-oriented service." in Sturdy, A., Grugulis, I. and Willmott, H., eds. *Customer Service: Empowerment and Entrapment*. London: Palgrave, 102-116.

Schramm, W. (ed.) (1963). *The Science of Human Communication*. Urbana, IL: University of Illinois Press.

Shannon, C. E., and Weaver, W. (1949/1963). *The Mathematical Theory of Communication*. Urbana, IL: University of Illinois Press.

Soros, G. (2000). *Open Society: Reforming Global Capitalism*. London: Little, Brown & Company.

Varey, R. J. (2002a). *Marketing Communication: Principles and Practice*. London: Routledge.

Varey, R. J. (2002b). *Relationship Marketing: Dialogue and Networks in the E-Commerce Era*. Chichester: Wiley.

Watzlawick, P., Beavin, J. H. and Jackson, D. H. (1967). *Pragmatics of Human Communication: A Study of Interactional Patterns, Pathologies, and Paradoxes*. New York: W. W. Norton.

Zuboff, S. (1988). *In the Age of the Smart Machine*. New York: Basic Books.

Trust, Satisfaction and Loyalty in Customer Relationship Management: An Application of Justice Theory

Lyle R. Wetsch

Memorial University, Canada

SUMMARY. In an attempt to increase customer loyalty amid increasingly competitive business environments, organizations are looking to customer relationship management (CRM) to help provide a solution. In spite of CRM failure rates cited as being as high as 70%, organizations continue to invest hundreds of thousands of dollars on CRM implementations. Attempts of past research to resolve why failure rates are so high have tended to focus on technological factors such as database integration or factors internal to the organization such as system adoption or organizational culture. While these areas are important, reactions of customers may also play a role. This paper uses justice theory to investigate the potential impact that customer involvement in a CRM implementation may have on customer loyalty. Propositions are provided to guide future research. *[Article copies available for a fee from The Haworth Document Delivery Service: 1-800-HAWORTH. E-mail address: <docdelivery@*

Lyle R. Wetsch, PhD, is Assistant Professor, Faculty of Business Administration, Memorial University, St. John's, Newfoundland, Canada (E-mail: LWetsch@mun.ca).

The author wishes to acknowledge the contributions and assistance provided by Dr. Peggy Cunningham and Dr. Brent Gallupe of Queen's University, Kingston, Ontario, Canada. Their ongoing support during the development of the ideas expressed within this paper is appreciated.

[Haworth co-indexing entry note]: "Trust, Satisfaction and Loyalty in Customer Relationship Management: An Application of Justice Theory." Wetsch, Lyle R. Co-published simultaneously in *Journal of Relationship Marketing* (Best Business Books, an imprint of The Haworth Press, Inc.) Vol. 4, No. 3/4, 2005, pp. 29-42; and: *The Future of Relationship Marketing* (ed: David Bejou, and Adrian Palmer) Best Business Books, an imprint of The Haworth Press, Inc., 2005, pp. 29-42. Single or multiple copies of this article are available for a fee from The Haworth Document Delivery Service [1-800-HAWORTH, 9:00 a.m. - 5:00 p.m. (EST). E-mail address: docdelivery@haworthpress.com].

29

KEYWORDS. CRM, justice, loyalty, customer relationship management, trust, customer voice, procedural justice

INTRODUCTION

It has been suggested that in an increasingly competitive environment characterised by rising customer recruitment costs, customer loyalty is the marketplace currency of the 21st century (Singh & Sirdeshmukh, 2000). Organizations are implementing technology based solutions such as customer relationship management (CRM) systems in the hope that they will improve productivity (McDonough, 2001), increase customer satisfaction (Burghard & Galimi, 2000) and increase profitability (Reichheld, 1996). Using CRM technologies in this quest for loyalty has not been cheap with investments in CRM related technologies expected to reach $12 billion in 2004 (Wardley & Shiang, 2000) and with 26% of US businesses spending in excess of $500,000 (US) each on CRM technology between 2002 and 2004 with some implementations up to $130 million US (Hellweg, 2002).

While CRM technologies can be used for many different applications such as handling call center enquiries and sales calls more efficiently and assisting in marketing programs, the application of interest in this paper is allowing organizations to better analyze customer data to provide customized products or services. Several practitioners have proposed that customer tailored products or services will add value for the customer and can lead to greater loyalty if firms make a commitment to do business on the customers terms (Flack & Evans, 2001).

Customer satisfaction has been increasing in the past few years although customer loyalty has been on the decline (Miller-Williams Inc., 2001) despite CRM system implementations. Existing CRM research has tended to focus on factors internal to the organization (Romano & Fjermestad, 2001) with a lack of studies investigating CRM implementations from the viewpoint of the end customer. The lack of customer focus extends to CRM implementations where many organizations have not solicited any customer input throughout the implementation process.

In the emerging customer-centric business environment (Keen, 1999), the power shift to the end consumer has placed certain elements of control over organizational success or failure in the consumers' hands. In spite of this, the customer has been relatively ignored in the current CRM research. This paper uses the theory of justice to investigate the proposed impact that customer involvement in a CRM implementation may have on customer loyalty.

The theory of justice has been researched for over 25 years in the organizational sciences (i.e., Colquitt, Conlon, Wesson, Porter, & Ng, 2001), marketing (i.e., Smith, Bolton, & Wagner, 1999; Tax, Brown, & Chandrashekaran, 1998), information systems (Hunton & Beeler, 1997) and performance appraisal systems (Nelson, 2001). The central concept of justice theory is consistent across disciplines. An organizations' actions are evaluated by customers/employees on the basis of justice (fairness) and customers/employees respond according to their fairness perceptions. This paper proposes that customers' fairness perceptions of an organization can be affected by a CRM implementation.

THEORETICAL BACKGROUND

Customer Relationship Management

The foundations for customer relationship management (CRM) can be found within several areas of marketing and management research including the original marketing concept, market orientation, and in the relationship marketing concept. That satisfied customers should be the main objective of business has been presented by several writers (i.e., Drucker, 1954; Felton, 1959). Although the customer was proposed to be at the center of the way organizations conducted business, the focus did not move from independent, discrete transactions focused on profit maximization until the 1980s (i.e., Dwyer, Schurr, & Oh, 1987).

MacNeil (1980) suggested that discrete transactions were rare and that marketing needed to begin to recognise the importance of ongoing buyer-seller relationships, or a series of relational exchanges. Relational exchanges are those that take place between two parties that have had past exchanges or who will have exchanges in the future (Anderson, 1995; Dwyer et al., 1987). The concept of relational exchange then led to the emergence of relationship marketing, a term first used by Berry (1983). Extensive research in relationship marketing was to follow in areas such as business-to-business or channel relationships (Morgan & Hunt, 1994), business-to-consumer relationships (Sheth & Parvatiyar, 1995), services marketing (Gronroos, 1990), and customers' relationships with brands (Fournier, Dobscha, & Mick, 1998). The shift to a customer focused approach or customer-centric marketing (Sheth, Sisodia, & Sharma, 2000) when combined with relationship marketing serve as the foundation for customer relationship management.

The important role of technology to customer relationship management is also found in the information systems (IS) field. Much of the foundation for CRM technologies can be found in the database, data mining, and decision support systems literature. Since 1984, more than 300 papers concerning ECCRM (Electronic Commerce Customer Relationship Management) have been published in the IS literature or by IS researchers (Romano, 2001).

Although an under researched area in the IS literature, some work is beginning to focus on how people interact with CRM technologies including the affective elements (Selz & Schubert, 1998) and virtual communities (Hagel & Armstrong, 1997). An emerging area of research in the IS field that has contributed to the study of customer relationship management is knowledge management. Examples of this work address issues ranging from online data collection (Sweeney, Soutar, Hausknecht, Dallin, & Johnson, 1997), people management (Swan, 2000), to customer power (Kannan, Chang, & Whinston, 1998). Marketing and IS research have at times overlapped during their evolution to customer relationship management. The concept of customer-centricity has been addressed in the marketing literature (Sheth et al., 2000), and in the IS literature Sweat (1999) described customer-centricity as being "about aligning a business to a customer's every need."

Despite its extensive research history, modern CRM requires additional research beyond traditional relationships with customers due to the increasing use of technology. Organizations have lost sight of the personal aspect of customer relationships and have begun to focus on the technology as the key for improving customer loyalty.

Loyalty

Loyalty is an elusive concept. In marketing literature, behavioural data is typically used to measure the loyalty of a customer because its collection is easier and less costly to obtain (Dekimpe, Steenkamp, Mellens, & Abeele, 1997). Behavioural data can include frequency of purchases, size of purchase, or share of wallet. The argument against behavioural data is that is it difficult to differentiate between spurious loyalty and true loyalty. Spurious loyalty involves a situation where the customer will migrate to alternatives at the first available opportunity.

True loyalty is the state where customers may never consider other options and may stay with an organization is spite of changes in factors such as price (Dick & Basu, 1994). Behavioural measures fail to distinguish between true and spurious loyalty and do not identify the factors that underlie the behaviour (Jacoby & Chestnut, 1978).

I base my definition of loyalty in the attitudinal context similar to that put forward by Oliver (1999). Loyalty is defined as a deeply held commitment to repatronize a product or service consistently in the future despite factors that may cause switching behaviour. Loyalty within organizations has been investigated by many researchers and a key theory that has been used to explain why customers are loyal is justice theory.

Justice Theory

There have been several types of justice proposed and evaluated in academic research; distributive justice (Adams, 1965), procedural justice (Thibaut & Walker, 1975), and interactional justice (Bies & Moag, 1986). Each of these has been found to have differential effects on individuals' perceptions of an organization.

Distributive justice has been defined as the perception that an individual holds of the fairness of the outcome (Adams, 1965). Assessments of distributive justice can be made using several means of evaluation including, equality, equity or need (Deutsch, 1975).

Interactional justice (Bies & Moag, 1986) has been defined by Novelli et al. (1995, p. 27) as the "perceived fairness of the interpersonal intervention received in a decision process". Interactional justice is thought to be more appropriately a reaction by individuals to agents (such as salespeople or supervisors) while procedural justice, which will be discussed next, is a reaction by individuals to decision making systems (i.e., organizations).

Procedural justice (Thibaut & Walker, 1975) is focused on the fairness of the process. Novelli et al. (1995, p. 25) defined procedural justice as "the perceived fairness of the methods or procedures used to determine who gets what outcomes, not the fairness of the outcomes themselves". The process is considered fair if there was adherence to fair criteria (Leventhal, 1980) or if the participants have process control through voice or influence (Folger, 1977; Lind & Tyler, 1988). There are three levels of voice that have been investigated (Hunton & Beeler, 1997); no voice, non-instrumental voice and instrumental voice.

In the organizational literature voice has been considered an antecedent to commitment or loyalty (Folger & Bies, 1989). In the IS and marketing literature voice has been investigated primarily as an antecedent to satisfaction (Bitner, Brown, & Meuter, 2000; Hunton & Beeler, 1997; Tax et al., 1998). Organizational literature has also indicated that procedural justice may have more impact on loyalty and distributive justice may be a more significant driver of satisfaction (Colquitt et al., 2001).

Based on anecdotal evidence several practitioner reports have suggested that there is a need for an increased level of customer participation in the CRM process (Malesiewski, 2001). Interviews with CRM consultants and organizations involved in implementing CRM systems indicate that a lack of customer involvement is one of the main problems today (Wetsch, 2004). It is this problem that is addressed in the research model and propositions in the next section.

RESEARCH MODEL AND PROPOSITIONS

The research model that has evolved from the customer relationship management, loyalty and justice theory literatures is presented in Figure 1. The focus of this model is on the effect that components of a CRM implementation (voice and value) will have on consumer's justice perceptions (distributive and procedural). Loyalty intention is proposed to be affected indirectly through satisfaction and trust.

Customer Value and Distributive Justice

Organizations have been developing strategies to increase the perceived value delivered to the customers (i.e., Reichheld, 1996). While there are several different definitions of value; it has been suggested that the most important evaluation (Webster, 1994) is an overall assessment of worth (Zeithaml, 1988) or subjective value. Subjective value is based on the benefits that the customer receives in relation to their sacrifices. In CRM implementations that result in a modification of products or services delivered to the customer, the value perception is based on the benefits that they have received in light of possible changes in the pricing structure or perceived service quality.

If the customer does not believe that they have received an increase in subjective value from the service provision adjustments, I propose that the customer will have a negative perception of the distributive justice that they have received. Reciprocally, if they receive an increase in subjective value, they will have a positive perception of the distributive jus-

FIGURE 1

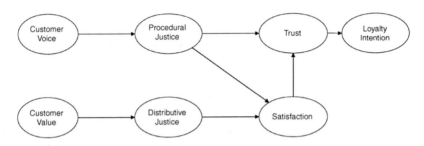

tice that they have received. The following is the proposed effect of customer subjective value perceptions:

P1: A higher level of perceived customer subjective value will lead to a higher level of distributive justice perception.

Customer Voice and Procedural Justice

Customer voice is the perceived degree of input that the customer has on changes that are taking place. Customers can have no voice or say in the decisions at all (no voice), a voice that is not taken into consideration (non-instrumental voice) or a voice that does appear to have been taken into consideration (instrumental voice). Research has suggested that the higher the level of instrumental voice, the higher the individuals' perceptions of procedural justice (Buttle, 1996; Folger, 1977; Leventhal, 1980; Lind & Tyler, 1988).

Anecdotal evidence suggests that the customer viewpoint is an important consideration during a CRM implementation (Blodgett, 2000; Donbavand, 2002). Actual practice suggests that the customer viewpoint has not generally been sought by organizations. Keen (1999) discussed the power shift to the customer and their increasing desire to have control. Providing customers with a voice by allowing them to provide input into the modification of products or services that they will receive will have a positive impact on their perception of procedural justice. I therefore propose the following effect of customer instrumental voice:

P2: A higher level of customer instrumental voice will lead to a higher level of procedural justice perception.

Distributive Justice and Overall Satisfaction

The impact that distributive justice has on trust and satisfaction has been one of the most studied elements of justice theory (i.e., Adams, 1965). Support for the link between distributive justice and satisfaction can be found in the organizational (Colquitt et al., 2001) and marketing literature (Szymanski & Henard, 2001).

Most satisfaction research has looked at transaction specific satisfaction (Oliver, 1993). Overall satisfaction based on total purchases and consumption with a good or service over a period of time has been suggested to be more appropriate to long term results such as loyalty (Anderson, Fornell, & Lehman, 1994). I propose that satisfaction based on an overall assessment as discussed by Garbarino and Johnson (1999) will be affected by a customers' distributive justice perceptions. I therefore propose the following effect on satisfaction:

> P3: A higher level of distributive justice perception held by a customer towards an organization will lead to a higher level of overall satisfaction.

Procedural Justice, Trust and Satisfaction

Procedural justice, or the perceived fairness of the process that has been undertaken (Thibaut & Walker, 1975), has been measured in many different ways (see justice theory meta-analysis conducted by Colquitt et al. (2001)). The early work by Thibaut and Walker (1975) focused on process control issues and this continues to appear as a proxy for procedural justice (Joy & Witt, 1992).

Organizational research on procedural justice has found that it has greater impact on trust and loyalty than other forms of justice such as distributive justice (Colquitt et al., 2001; Hunton & Beeler, 1997; Kim & Mauborgne, 1997). There is considerably less research on the relationship between procedural justice perceptions and trust than with other dependent variables (Colquitt et al., 2001). Holmes and Rempel (1989) have stated that trust is strengthened by acknowledging an individual's particular needs and affirming their sense of worth.

I believe that the customer's sense of worth will be increased when they perceive a high level of procedural justice. I therefore propose the following effect of procedural justice on trust:

P4: A higher level of procedural justice perceptions held by a customer towards an organization will lead to increased trust.

While procedural justice perception appears to be more predictive of trust and distributive justice perception appears to be more predictive of satisfaction (McFarlin & Sweeney, 1992), some studies have found that procedural justice also has an effect on satisfaction in the workplace (Greenberg, 1986). Although not widely investigated in the customer satisfaction literature, there have been a few studies that have found support for a link between procedural justice and customer satisfaction (Tax et al., 1998; Teo & Lim, 2001).

I propose that the trust that an individual feels toward an organization is increased by the procedural justice perception held by the individual. This occurs both directly (as was addressed in P4) as well as indirectly through an increase in overall satisfaction that the customer feels toward the organization. Therefore I propose the following:

P5: A higher level of procedural justice perceptions held by a customer towards an organization will lead to increased overall satisfaction with the organization.

Overall Satisfaction and Trust

Customer satisfaction has become a central focus of business operations and a main focus of academic research. Findings on the effects of satisfaction have been mixed and sometimes contradictory (Szymanski & Henard, 2001). Specifically the link between customer satisfaction and loyalty suggested by Oliver (1999) is potentially mediated by other constructs such as trust. Some of the conflicting results may be due to studies that have evaluated encounter specific satisfaction and tried to link this with more long-term cumulative constructs such as trust or loyalty. Ganesan (1994) suggested that satisfaction over time reinforces the perceived reliability of the firm and contributes to trust. Therefore, overall satisfaction accumulated over time (Anderson et al., 1994) should have a stronger relationship with trust than encounter specific satisfaction. I therefore propose the following relationship between overall satisfaction and trust:

P6: Overall customer satisfaction with an organization is positively related to trust.

Trust and Loyalty Intention

Trust has been generally accepted as a critical element in positive relationships (Moorman, Zaltman, & Deshpande, 1992; Morgan & Hunt, 1994). Trust is especially important in relationship marketing (Gronroos, 1990). The outcomes of developing trust include increasing customer loyalty (Garbarino & Johnson, 1999), relationship commitment (Dwyer et al., 1987) as well as profitability (Doney & Cannon, 1997). Organizational research has also shown that trust has a positive effect on loyalty in organizations and may indeed be more critical to loyalty than satisfaction (Colquitt et al., 2001; Kim & Mauborgne, 1997). I therefore propose the following relationship between trust and loyalty intention:

> P7: The trust that a consumer has for an organization is positively related to loyalty intention.

DISCUSSION

This paper has presented a model for CRM success based on justice theory. The model presented in this paper is currently under empirical study to validate the conceptual relationships that have been presented. The finished work will contribute to our knowledge in the areas of customer relationship management and service customization by evaluating the impact of providing a customer with a voice in the customization of products or services. Additionally, this research will provide additional insight into the satisfaction-loyalty-trust relationships.

For organizations that implement CRM programs, the findings of this research will enable them to determine the impact of allowing customers to have a voice in the customization of their goods or services. Also the impact of perceived value will be better understood. The findings will also allow organizations to determine the role of overall satisfaction and trust in determining a customers' loyalty intention.

Future research could address the impact that offering the customer a voice and then not delivering will have on their attitudes. This will allow organizations to understand the risks that are involved with giving customers the offer of customer input and then ignoring this input (non-instrumental voice)–a situation that can occur with some CRM implementations. The findings of his research may apply not only to CRM but also to any situation where the organisation is planning on providing customized products or services.

REFERENCES

Adams, J. S. (1965). Inequity in Social Exchange. In L. Berkowitz (Ed.), *Advances in Experimental Social Psychology* (Vol. 2). New York: Academic Press.

Anderson, E. W., Fornell, C., & Lehman, D. (1994). Customer Satisfaction, Market Share, and Profitability: Findings from Sweden. *Journal of Marketing, 58*(July), 53-66.

Anderson, J. C. (1995). Relationships in Business Markets: Exchange Episodes, Value Creation, and Their Empirical Assessment. *Journal of the Academy of Marketing Science, 23*(4), 346-350.

Berry, L. L. (1983). Relationship Marketing. In L. L. Berry, G. L. Shostack & G. Upah (Eds.), *Emerging Perspectives on Services Marketing* (pp. 25-28). Chicago: American Marketing Association.

Bies, R. J., & Moag, J. F. (1986). Interactional Justice: Communication Criteria of Fairness. In R. J. Lewicki, B. H. Sheppard & M. H. Bazerman (Eds.), *Research on Negotiations in Organizations* (Vol. 1, pp. 43-55). Grennwich, CT: JAI Press.

Bitner, M. J., Brown, S. W., & Meuter, M. L. (2000). Technology Infusion in Service Encounters. *Journal of the Academy of Marketing Science, 28*(1), 138-149.

Blodgett, M. (2000). Masters of the Customer Connection. *CIO Magazine, August.*

Burghard, C., & Galimi, J. (2000). Customer Relationship Management-New MCO Catalyst. *Gartner Advisory, January.*

Buttle, F. (1996). Unserviceable Concepts in Service Marketing. *The Quarterly Review of Marketing, 11*(3), 8-14.

Colquitt, J. A., Conlon, D. E., Wesson, M. J., Porter, C. O. L. H., & Ng, K. Y. (2001). Justice in the Millennium: A Meta-Analytic Review of 25 years of Organizational Justice Research. *Journal of Applied Psychology, 86*(3), 425-445.

Dekimpe, M. G., Steenkamp, J.-B. E. M., Mellens, M., & Abeele, P. V. (1997). Decline and Variability in Brand Loyalty. *International journal of Research in Marketing, 14*(5), 405-420.

Deutsch, M. (1975). Equity, Equality and Need: What Determines Which Value Will be Used as the Basis for Distribution Justice. *Journal of Social Issues, 31*(3), 137-149.

Dick, A. S., & Basu, K. (1994). Customer Loyalty: Toward an Integrated Conceptual Framework. *Journal of the Academy of Marketing Science, 22*, 99-113.

Donbavand, R. (2002). Using Innovative Research to Build the Foundations of Actionable CRM Strategies. *Interactive Marketing, 3*(3), 243-253.

Doney, P. M., & Cannon, J. P. (1997). An Examination of the Nature of Trust in Buyer-Seller Relationships. *Journal of Marketing, 61*(April), 35-51.

Drucker, P. (1954). *The Practice of Management.* New York: Harper and Row Publishers.

Dwyer, R. F., Schurr, P. H., & Oh, S. (1987). Developing Buyer-Seller Relationships. *Journal of Marketing, 51*(April), 11-27.

Felton, A. P. (1959). Making the Marketing Concept Work. *Harvard Business Review, 37*(4), 55-65.

Flack, D., & Evans, P. (2001). Marketing on Customer Terms. *Marketing Management,* 19-23.

Folger, R. (1977). Distributive and Procedural Justice: Combined Impact of "Voice" and Improvement on Experienced Inequity. *Journal of Personality and Social Psychology, 35*, 108-119.

Folger, R., & Bies, R. J. (1989). Managerial Responsibilities and Procedural Justice. *Employee Responsibility and Rights Journal, 2*(2), 79-90.

Fournier, S., Dobscha, S., & Mick, D. G. (1998). Preventing the premature death of relationship marketing. *Harvard Business Review, 76*(1), 42&.

Ganesan, S. (1994). Determinants of Long-term Orientation in Buyer-Seller Relationships. *Journal of Marketing, 58*(2), 1-19.

Garbarino, E., & Johnson, M. S. (1999). The different roles of satisfaction, trust, and commitment in customer relationships. *Journal of Marketing, 63*(2), 70-87.

Greenberg, J. (1986). Determinants of Perceived Fairness of Performance Evaluations. *Journal of Applied Psychology, 71*(2), 340-342.

Gronroos, C. (1990). Relationship Approach to Marketing in Service Contexts: The Marketing and the Organizational Behaviour Interface. *Journal of Business Research, 20*(1), 3-11.

Hagel, J., & Armstrong, A. G. (1997). *Net Gain: Expanding Markets Through Virtual Communities.* Boston: Harvard Business School Press.

Hellweg, E. (2002). CRM Success: Still the Exception, Not the Rule. *Business 2.0, July.*

Holmes, J. G., & Rempel, J. K. (1989). Trust in Close Relationships. In C. Hendrick (Ed.), *Review of Personality and Social Psychology: Close Relationships* (Vol. 10, pp. 187-220). Beverly Hills, CA: Sage Publications.

Hunton, J. E., & Beeler, J. D. (1997). Effects of User Participation in Systems Development: A Longitudinal Field Experiment. *MIS Quarterly, 21*(4), 359-388.

Jacoby, J., & Chestnut, R. W. (1978). *Brand Loyalty: Measurement and Management.* Chichester: New York: Wiley.

Joy, V. L., & Witt, L. A. (1992). Delay of Gratification as a Moderator of the Procedural Justice-Distributive Justice Relationship. *Group and Organization Management, 17*, 297-308.

Kannan, P. K., Chang, A.-M., & Whinston, A. (1998). Marketing Information of the I-Way. *Communications of the ACM, 41*(3), 35-43.

Keen, P. G. W. (1999). *Competing in Chapter 2 of Internet Business.* Delft, The Netherlands: Eburon.

Kim, W. C., & Mauborgne, R. (1997). Fair Process: Managing in the Knowledge Economy. *Harvard Business Review, July-August.*

Leventhal, G. S. (1980). What Should Be Done With Equity Theory? New Approaches to the Study of Fairness in Social Relationships. In K. Gergen, M. Greenberg & R. Willis (Eds.), *Social Exchange: Advances in Theory and Research* (pp. 27-55). New York: Plenum.

Lind, E. A., & Tyler, T. R. (1988). *The Social Psychology of Procedural Justice.* New York: Plenum.

MacNeil, I. R. (1980). *The New Social Contract.* London: Yale University Press.

Malesiewski, S. (2001). Re-thinking the Mysterious CRM. *Integrated Solutions* (January).

McDonough, D. (2001, October 22, 2001). How CRM Can Save The Economy. *CRM Daily.*

McFarlin, D. B., & Sweeney, P. D. (1992). Distributive and Procedural Justice as Predictors of Satisfaction With Personal and Organizational Outcomes. *Academy of Management Journal, 35*(3), 626-637.

Miller-Williams Inc. (2001). *The Customer Satisfaction-Loyalty trap* (White Paper). San Diego: Miller-Williams Inc.

Moorman, C., Zaltman, G., & Deshpande, R. (1992). Relationships Between Providers and users of Market Research: The Dynamics of Trust Within and Between Organizations. *Journal of Marketing Research, 29*(August), 314-328.

Morgan, R. M., & Hunt, S. D. (1994). The Commitment-Trust Theory of Relationship Marketing. *Journal of Marketing, 58*(July), 20-38.

Nelson, K. G. (2001). *Toward a Comprehensive Model of Telecommuter Adjustment.* Paper presented at the 2001-Seventh Americas Conference on Information Systems.

Novelli, L., Kirkman, B. L., & Shapiro, D. L. (1995). Effective Implementation of Organizational Change: An Organizational Justice Perspective. In C. L. Cooper & D. M. Rousseau (Eds.), *Trends in Organizational Behaviour.* New York, NY: John Wiley & Sons Ltd.

Oliver, R. (1999). Whence Consumer Loyalty. *Journal of Marketing, 63*(Special Issue), 33-44.

Oliver, R. L. (1993). Cognitive, Affective, and Attribute Bases of the Satisfaction Response. *Journal of Consumer Research, 20*(December), 418-430.

Reichheld, F. F. (1996). *The Loyalty Effect.* Cambridge, MA: Harvard Business School Press.

Romano, N. C. (2001). *Customer Relations Management Research: An Assessment of Sub Field Development and Maturity.* Paper presented at the 34th Hawaii International Conference on Systems Science, Maui, Hawaii.

Romano, N. C., & Fjermestad, J. (2001). *An Agenda for Electronic Commerce Customer Relationship Management Research.* Paper presented at the Seventh Americas Conference on Information Systems (AMCIS), Boston.

Selz, D., & Schubert, P. (1998). *Web Assessment: A Model for the Evaluation and the Assessment of Successful Electronic Commerce Applications.* Paper presented at the HICSS, Maui, Hawaii.

Sheth, J. N., & Parvatiyar, A. (1995). Relationship Marketing in Consumer Markets: Antecedents and Consequences. *Journal of the Academy of Marketing Science, 23*(4), 255-271.

Sheth, J. N., Sisodia, R. S., & Sharma, A. (2000). The antecedents and consequences of customer-centric marketing. *Journal of the Academy of Marketing Science, 28*(1), 55-66.

Singh, J., & Sirdeshmukh, D. (2000). Agency and Trust Mechanisms in Consumer Satisfaction and Loyalty Judgements. *Journal of the Academy of Marketing Science, 28*(1), 150-167.

Smith, A. K., Bolton, R. N., & Wagner, J. (1999). A Model of Customer Satisfaction with Service Encounters Involving Failure and Recovery. *Journal of Marketing Research, 36*(August), 356-372.

Swan, J. (2000). *Knowledge Management in Action: Integrating Knowledge Across Communities.* Paper presented at the HICSS, Maui, Hawaii.

Sweat, J. (1999). Customer Centricity in the Post Y2K Era. *Information Week, 734,* 46-62.

Sweeney, J. C., Soutar, G. N., Hausknecht, D. R., Dallin, R. F., & Johnson, L. W. (1997). Collecting Information From Groups: A Comparison of Two Methods. *Journal of the Market Research Society, 39*(2), 397-411.

Szymanski, D. M., & Henard, D. H. (2001). Customer Satisfaction: A Meta-Analysis of the Empirical Evidence. *Journal of the Academy of Marketing Science, 29*(1), 16-35.

Tax, S. S., Brown, S. W., & Chandrashekaran, M. (1998). Customer Evaluations of Service Complaint Experiences: Implications for Relationship Marketing. *Journal of Marketing, 62*(April), 60-77.

Teo, T. S. H., & Lim, V. K. G. (2001). The Effects of Perceived Justice on Satisfaction and Behavioural Intentions: The Case of Computer Purchase. *International Journal of Retail and Distribution Management, 29*(2), 109-124.

Thibaut, J., & Walker, L. (1975). *Procedural Justice: A Psychological Analysis.* Hillsdale, NJ: Erlbaum.

Wardley, M., & Shiang, D. (2000). Customer Relationship Management Market Forecast and Analysis, 2000-2004". *IDC,* 1-119.

Webster, F. E. (1994). Defining the New Marketing Concept. *Marketing Management, 2*(4), 23-31.

Wetsch, L. R. (2004). Spelling Customer Relationship Management with a Small 'c'; Thoughts from the World of Business. *Work in Progress.*

Zeithaml, V. (1988). Consumer Perceptions of Price, Quality, and Value: A Means-End Model and Synthesis of Evidence. *Journal of Marketing, 52*(3), 2-22.

Are Variety-Seekers Bad Customers? An Analysis of the Role of Recommendations in the Service Profit Chain

Herbert Woratschek

University of Bayreuth, Germany

Chris Horbel

University of Bayreuth, Germany

SUMMARY. Variety-seeking behavior occurs if customers derive utility from a change of service providers. It has negative consequences for the firm's profits, because it functions as a moderating factor in the relationship of customer satisfaction and customer loyalty. Even by offering high service quality variety-seekers cannot be retained. Therefore variety-seekers are often seen as "bad" customers, because they are not loyal to the firm. This article will show variety-seeking behavior in a more positive light. Variety-seekers are satisfied customers and therefore they are likely to engage in positive

Dr. Herbert Woratschek, PhD, is Professor and Chair, Services Management, University of Bayreuth, 95440 Bayreuth, Germany (E-mail: dlm@uni-bayreuth.de).

Diplomkauffrau Chris Horbel, PhD, is Research Assistant and PhD student, Department of Services Management, University of Bayreuth, 95440 Bayreuth, Germany (E-mail: chris.horbel@uni-bayreuth.de).

[Haworth co-indexing entry note]: "Are Variety-Seekers Bad Customers? An Analysis of the Role of Recommendations in the Service Profit Chain." Woratschek, Herbert, and Chris Horbel. Co-published simultaneously in *Journal of Relationship Marketing* (Best Business Books, an imprint of The Haworth Press, Inc.) Vol. 4, No. 3/4, 2005, pp. 43-57; and: *The Future of Relationship Marketing* (ed: David Bejou, and Adrian Palmer) Best Business Books, an imprint of The Haworth Press, Inc., 2005, pp. 43-57. Single or multiple copies of this article are available for a fee from The Haworth Document Delivery Service [1-800-HAWORTH, 9:00 a.m. - 5:00 p.m. (EST). E-mail address: docdelivery@haworthpress.com].

word-of-mouth communication. Recommendations will help to attract new customers and thus increase profits. *[Article copies available for a fee from The Haworth Document Delivery Service: 1-800-HAWORTH. E-mail address: <docdelivery@haworthpress.com> Website: <http://www.HaworthPress. com> © 2005 by The Haworth Press, Inc. All rights reserved.]*

KEYWORDS. Variety-seeking behavior, word-of-mouth, opinion leadership, customer satisfaction

RELATIONSHIP MARKETING IN SERVICES

In services marketing it is widely postulated that improvement in service quality, as perceived by the customer, will lead to an increase in customer satisfaction, loyalty, and profits (Gummesson, 2001; Heskett, Sasser & Schlesinger, 1997). However, the concept of relationship marketing evolved from the notion that the outcome of higher profits from high service quality is not automatic. The service provider must invest in the development and maintenance of customer relationships to make them sustaining and thus profitable (Grönroos, 1990; Morgan & Hunt, 1994). In other words, "effective relationship marketing should help a company capitalize on its investment in service improvement" (Berry, 1995, p. 237).

Relationship marketing benefits both, the firm and the customer. Concerning benefits for the firm, it has been demonstrated in a number of studies that profits increase when customer loyalty increases (Heskett, Jones, Loveman, Sasser, & Schlesinger, 1994).

However, long-term relationships to a service provider are often also valuable to the customer. Services are difficult to evaluate prior to the purchase. For example, the immateriality of services and the uncertainty about the capabilities of the market partner and its willingness to serve leads to high market uncertainty (Woratschek & Horbel, 2002). The high degree of purchase risk encourages customers to remain with service providers they trust (Zeithaml & Bitner, 2000). Relationships are valuable to customers as they reduce the risks involved in purchasing services (Berry, 2002). Many services are also characterized by a high degree of individuality and the integration of the customer into the production process (Woratschek & Horbel, 2002). Repeatedly providing a service to the same customer helps the supplier to learn more about the customer's requirements and hence, to tailor the service to the customer's specific needs (Berry, 2002). Close interaction between the customer and a key contact employee on the supplier's side is often necessary (Zeithaml & Bitner, 2000). Customers can obtain social benefits from these relationships as they sometimes even form friendships with their service providers (Price & Arnould, 1999).

As a result, benefits from relationship marketing on the firm's as well as on the customer's side seem to be immense. However, there are service industries where we can observe only a low degree of customer loyalty, although the risk involved in these services is high. For example, deciding on a holiday destination involves high risk for a tourist if he does not know the destination and the service providers at the destination from a former vacation. Still, many people tend to travel to a different place each time they go on holiday. For example, in one of our empirical investigations in the popular German destination Garmisch-Partenkirchen, 75% of the tourists answered that they were very satisfied with their vacation, but only 33% planned to return. Such behavior is referred to as variety-seeking behavior. Customers might derive utility from a change of a service provider, and therefore switch to another provider at the next purchase (Givon, 1984).

This leads to negative consequences for the service providers at the destination, because the attraction of new guests is very expensive. Variety-seeking customers are therefore often seen as "bad" customers, because even offering very high service quality does not make them loyal customers. As a consequence, "relationship marketing's central idea-market to existing customers so that they become *better*, more loyal customers" (Berry, 2002, p. 71), is not applicable to variety-seeking customers.

Despite the mentioned negative consequences of variety-seeking behavior for relationship marketing, we will show that there are also positive aspects of this behavior. We will therefore introduce recommendations as one possible instrument of relationship marketing to reduce the mentioned negative effects of variety-seeking behavior.

THE SERVICE PROFIT CHAIN

The impact of service quality on profits and other financial outcomes of a firm has received considerable attention in marketing theory (Rust, Zahorik, & Keiningham, 1995). The way to achieve financial success in a service firm can be illustrated in the service profit chain. It shows the relationships between employee satisfaction, perceived service quality, customer satisfaction, customer loyalty and higher long-term profits (Heskett et al., 1997).

In services management it is often postulated that the customer's perception of service quality drives customer satisfaction (Zeithaml & Bitner, 2000). Satisfied customers repeatedly buy products and services. They become loyal customers (Heskett et al., 1994). Customer loyalty provides the basis for the development of long-term relationships with customers. These lead to higher revenues through increasing purchases and lower costs, thus profits will increase (Zeithaml & Bitner, 2000).

Further, personnel plays an important role for the delivery of services. The abilities and motivation of service employees have an important impact on customer orientation which is directly linked to customer satisfaction (Boles, Babin, Brashear, & Brooks, 2001). Therefore, employee satisfaction is necessary to reach customer satisfaction, customer loyalty, and increased profits.

However, research on the service profit chain has highlighted the fact that these relationships are not always simple (Zeithaml, Berry, & Parasuraman, 1996). Investment of companies in improvements of service quality do not automatically lead to improved economic success (Zeithaml et al., 1996). There are factors moderating the relationships shown in Figure 1. Variety-seeking behavior, on which we will have a closer look in this article, is one of these factors. If vari-

FIGURE 1. The Service Profit Chain

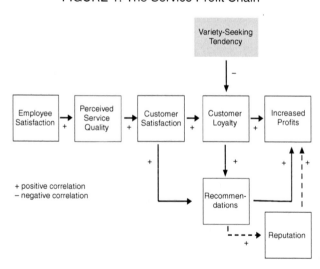

ety-seeking behavior occurs, the relationship between customer satisfaction and loyalty is ambivalent, because variety-seeking tendency is negatively correlated with customer loyalty.

As variety-seeking consumers will choose another service provider at the next purchase, one could argue that it is unnecessary to provide high service quality to these consumers. High service quality leads to high costs and variety-seekers will not generate future revenues, thus profits will decrease.

However, there is not only one way leading from customer satisfaction to higher long-term profits. There is wide agreement that highly satisfied customers are likely to engage in positive word-of-mouth communication (Bone, 1992). Positive word-of-mouth communication will attract new customers and, hence, lead to higher revenues. Moreover, recommendations help to build-up reputation of a company, which will also increase profits in the long run.

We further assume that recommendations increase with higher customer loyalty, because loyal customers feel more attached to the service provider. Therefore, it is not clear which influence variety-seeking behavior of customers has on their word-of-mouth communication behavior. We assume that the effect of customer satisfaction on recommendations is stronger than the effect of variety-seeking tendency, because there is also a positive correlation between the degree of satisfaction of variety-seekers and recommendations.

VARIETY-SEEKING BEHAVIOR OF SERVICE CUSTOMERS

This paper is focused on variety-seeking behavior as one moderating factor in the service profit chain. Variety-seeking behavior of consumers has received considerable attention in marketing literature (e.g., Faison, 1977; Givon, 1984; Hoyer & Ridgway, 1984; McAlister & Pessemier, 1982). Variety-seeking behavior results from the simple desire for change. It is "switching for the sake of variety" (McAlister, 1982, p. 141). To Givon (1984) variety-seeking (or avoidance) behavior is "the phenomenon of an individual consumer switching brands (or repeat buying) induced by the utility (or dis-utility) she derives from the change itself irrespective of the brands she switches to or from" (p. 2).

However, the focus of past research has been on consumer goods. Although Hirschman and Wallendorf (1980) state that people may exhibit variety-seeking behavior in several areas of their lives, variety-seeking behavior in services markets has not received very much attention yet.

However, we believe that variety-seeking behavior might be even more important for services management.

This paper contributes to the existing literature as we show the important impact of variety-seeking behavior on one service industry. In tourism variety-seeking behavior is a very relevant phenomenon as many people switch the destination each time they go on holiday, because they simply want to see something else. In this industry, different types of variety-seeking behavior might occur:

1. Variety-seeking behavior among different sport and leisure activities at a destination.
2. Variety-seeking behavior among different destinations.
3. Variety-seeking behavior among different types of vacation.

From the perspective of the destination manager, a restaurant, a hotel or any other service provider at a particular destination, only the first type can relatively easily be managed by offering a broad variety of activities. The second and third type have serious consequences. Even offering very high service quality will not help to make these variety-seeking tourists come back. The relevant question for the service providers concerned is: What can be done to make the best out of that situation? We will have a closer look on the word-of-mouth communication behavior of variety-seekers to answer that question.

EMPIRICAL STUDY

Research Design and Hypotheses

The empirical study was one part of a larger research project in the popular German destination Garmisch-Partenkirchen in Winter 2001/02. The overall study was aimed at getting a better understanding of the influences of tourists' decision for a destination, of the determinants of customer satisfaction and customer loyalty in tourism, as well as of the influences of the duration of stay of tourists at a destination.

This piece of research has another objective. It is focused on the relevance of variety-seeking behavior and recommendations within the service profit chain. Within two periods of time a total of 428 personal interviews with tourists were conducted, whereby standardized questionnaires were used. The age quota was linked to the official registration statistics.

In our empirical study we focus on one part of the service profit chain. The following hypotheses are of interest.

H1: Customer satisfaction is positively correlated with recommendations.

H2: Customer loyalty is expected to increase as customer satisfaction increases.

H3: Recommendations are expected to increase as customer loyalty increases.

H4: Variety-seeking tendency should be negatively correlated to customer loyalty.

H5: The influence of customer satisfaction on recommendations is stronger than that of variety-seeking tendency.

Table 1 contains the indicators used to measure the variables.

As we conducted the study in only one period of time, our indicators for the variables measure only behavioral intentions instead of observed behavior. As the original objective of the overall study was different from the focus of this article, we can only measure one indicator for each variable.

Results

All variables were measured on a 5-point scale ('not satisfied at all' to 'extraordinarily satisfied' for overall customer satisfaction and 'strongly agree' to 'strongly disagree' for customer loyalty, recommendations and variety-seeking tendency).

TABLE 1. Indicators for Variables

Variable	Indicator
Customer Satisfaction	How satisfied are you in general with your holiday in Garmisch-Partenkirchen?
Customer Loyalty	I will definitely spend at least one holiday in Garmisch-Partenkirchen within the next 3 years.
Recommendations	I am happy to recommend Garmisch-Partenkirchen as a holiday destination.
Variety-Seeking Tendency	I travel to a different place each time I go on holiday.

Hypotheses 1 to 4 were tested using correlation analysis. All correlations are statistically highly significant (p < 0,001), thus supporting the hypotheses. Figure 2 shows the correlation coefficients.

The correlation analysis could not answer the question which effect consumer's variety-seeking tendency has on recommendations. We therefore used a regression model to investigate this relationship, which is stated in hypothesis 5. 'Recommendations' was used as the dependent variable and customer satisfaction and variety-seeking tendency as the independent variables. The model was statistically highly significant. Table 2 contains the regression coefficients.

An examination of the results shows that the positive influence of customer satisfaction on recommendations is much stronger than the negative influence of variety-seeking tendency, thus supporting hypothesis 5. Hence, customer satisfaction influences recommendation much more than variety-seeking tendency.

WORD-OF-MOUTH COMMUNICATION
OF DIFFERENT CUSTOMER SEGMENTS

Our empirical example confirms our assumed correlations in the service profit chain. Based on the findings from the empirical study we

FIGURE 2. Correlation Coefficients

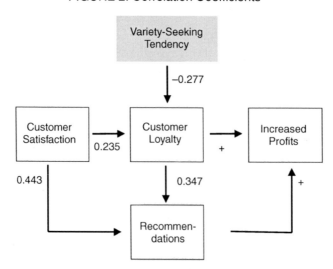

TABLE 2. Regression Results

	Beta	Beta stand.	Probability	95%-c. interv.	VIF
Customer satisfaction	0.612	0.449	p < 0.001	0.492/0.733	1.003
Variety seeking-tendency	−0.074	−0.097	p < 0.001	−0.142/−0.007	1.003
R^2 = 0.206 Adj. R^2 = 0.202 Dependent variable: recommendation					

identified four segments of customers who need to be considered concerning their word-of-mouth communication behavior. We therefore divided our sample of tourists on the basis of the variables customer satisfaction and variety-seeking tendency as shown in Figure 3.

Over 30 percent of the tourists have been relatively dissatisfied with their vacation in Garmisch-Partenkirchen. These customers are a potential danger as they are likely to engage in negative word-of-mouth communication, which can cause severe damage (Richins, 1983). In particular, dissatisfied movers or "terrorists" (Jones & Sasser, 1995, p. 96) are likely to engage in negative word-of-mouth because they travel around and talk a lot to potential customers about their experiences. The so-called "hostages" (Jones & Sasser, 1995, p. 97) seem to be attached to the destination. Therefore, they might not be very likely to spread negative word-of-mouth, but, the probability of positive word-of-mouth communication of these guests is also relatively low. Both groups of satisfied tourists are more or less likely to make recommendations. In the regression analysis we could further see that the probability of a person to make a favorable recommendation is higher if variety-seeking tendency is lower–given the same level of customer satisfaction. Therefore, "loyalists" (Jones & Sasser, 1995, p. 96) will possibly be more likely to make a recommendation than variety-seeking tourists, which might also be due to the fact that they feel more attached to the destination.

However, one could argue that a variety-seeking tourist meets more people because he spends every holiday in another destination. In general, variety-seekers might meet more people because they change shopping locations more frequently, go to many different places to spend their spare time, etc.

This is consistent with the notion that variety-seeking behavior also depends on personal characteristics. People's cultural backgrounds,

FIGURE 3. Word-of-Mouth Communication Behavior of Different Customer Segments

Variety-Seeking Tendency / Customer Satisfaction	Low (1-3)	High (4-5)
Low (1-3)	Resigned Inertia Tourists "Hostages" (26.02%)	Dissatisfied Movers "Terrorists" (5.30%)
High (4-5)	Satisfied Inertia Tourists "Loyalists"/"Apostles" (57.35%)	Variety-Seeking-Tourists "Mercenaries" (11.33%)

ideological attitudes and their lifestyles influence their variety-seeking tendency. People dedicated to a rather Spartan life are less likely to engage in variety-seeking behavior than people living a hedonistic lifestyle (van Trijp, Hoyer, & Inman, 1996). Venturesome, spontaneous and creative people will as well have a higher tendency to show variety-seeking behavior than risk-averse, rational people (Hoyer & Ridgway, 1984). Thus, possibly, variety-seeking consumers are more communicative (Raju, 1980; McAlister & Pessemier, 1982).

If variety-seekers really are more communicative, one could assume that they have more contacts with potential customers of the firm who they can tell about the experience. As Figure 4 shows, the number of recommendations a satisfied customer makes might as well depend on the number of potential customers the person meets as on the personal probability of this person to engage in favorable word-of-mouth communication. In our example, variety-seeking tourists are traveling around more and hence they are likely to talk to a lot of other tourists that prefer the same type of destination. These tourists have a high potential to become guests of the destination concerned.

In order to estimate how valuable recommendations are, it would be necessary to know how many of the recommendations lead to the acquisition of a new customer. In our study, the proportion of people who

FIGURE 4. Influences on Recommendations

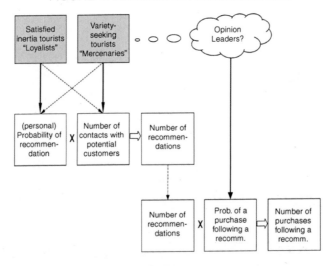

came to Garmisch-Partenkirchen because of a recommendation of friends or relatives was relatively high (37.9%). Further, one has to take into account that some people have more influence than others. Recommendations of opinion leaders lead with a higher probability to a purchase than recommendations of other people.

As variety-seeking tourists have already seen a lot of destinations, they might be seen as experts in tourism. Hence, it is likely that they function as opinion leaders, because they have more knowledge about the subject than others (Chaney, 2001). Moreover, our literature review showed that past research revealed some characteristics of variety-seekers which are quite similar to some characteristics of opinion leaders. For example, members of both groups seem to be more venturesome, innovative and gregarious (Baumgarten, 1975; Hirschman & Wallendorf, 1980; Hoyer & Ridgway, 1984; Myers & Robertson, 1972; Raju, 1980; Summers, 1970; Taylor, 1977). Other research (Table 3) indicates that they are characterized by higher levels of income and education (Gatignon & Robertson, 1985; McAlister & Pessemier, 1982; Raju, 1980). They also seem to strive for more individuality in public environments (Chan & Misra, 1990; Ratner & Kahn, 2002).

If the similarities between variety-seeking consumers and opinion leaders exist, variety-seeking consumers are even more valuable for a firm. However, usually the total mix of communication instruments as

TABLE 3. Characteristics of Variety-Seekers and Opinion Leaders

Characteristics of variety-seeking consumers	Characteristics of opinion leaders
venturesome (Raju, 1980)	higher risk-preference (Taylor, 1977)
extrovert (Hoyer & Ridgway, 1984)	gregarious (Baumgarten, 1975), socially active (Summers, 1970)
innovative (Hirschman & Wallendorf, 1980)	innovative (Summers, 1970; Myers & Robertson, 1972)
higher level of education (Raju, 1980; McAllister & Pessemier, 1982)	higher level of education (Gatignon & Robertson, 1985)
higher level of income (Raju, 1980; McAllister & Pessemier, 1982)	higher level of income (Gatignon & Robertson, 1985)
affinity to socially conspicuous products (Ratner & Kahn, 2002)	higher degree of public individuation (Chan & Misra, 1990)

well as other factors (e.g., family) will influence the decision to spend vacation in one particular destination, or in general, to buy a particular product or service. Therefore, further research is necessary to better understand the weight of the influence of recommendations.

CONCLUSION

Variety-seeking behavior leads to negative consequences for the service provider, because even offering very high service quality to these consumers will not make them loyal customers. Therefore, variety-seeking customers are widely seen as "bad" customers. Through an analysis of their word-of-mouth communication behavior we have shown variety-seeking consumers in a more positive light.

Our empirical study revealed that the positive influence of satisfaction on recommendations is much stronger than the negative influence of variety-seeking tendency. We have discussed that recommendations of variety-seekers might be valuable for gaining new customers. As they probably meet potential customers, they can give a lot of relevant recommendations. Moreover, they might be seen as experts, because they can compare many different service providers. Their possible expert status, and the outcome of our literature review that they seem to have some characteristics that are similar to some characteristics of opinion leaders, led us to the assumption that they might be opinion leaders.

As a result, word-of-mouth communication of variety-seekers might compensate the negative consequences of variety-seeking behavior. Therefore, management of customer satisfaction should be given top priority to generate positive word-of-mouth. As a result we assume that variety-seekers are not "bad" customers, just because they are not loyal. They are "good" customers, because they build up reputation of a destination or a company.

Several limitations of our empirical example in the tourism industry must be recognized. The results may not be transferable to other service industries. Further, the variables were mainly behavioral intentions rather than actual behavior, and hence, the results of this study must be interpreted with caution.

Future research concerning recommendations as an instrument to reduce the negative consequences of variety-seeking behavior is necessary. The value of recommendations for the acquisition of new customers should be investigated, because the weight of the influence of recommendations on acquisition determines profits. Moreover, empirical and theoretical research is necessary to find out whether variety-seekers are really more communicative and if they function as opinion leaders. If this were true variety-seekers could be "better" word-of-mouth communicators than loyal customers.

If recommendations are valuable, it remains a question, what management can do to induce customers to spread positive word-of-mouth. Therefore, deeper insights on the antecedents of word-of-mouth communication behavior and on how to influence opinion leaders are necessary.

REFERENCES

Baumgarten, S. A. (1975). The Innovative Consumer in the Diffusion Process. *Journal of Marketing Research, 12*(1), 12-18.

Berry, L. L. (1995). Relationship Marketing of Services-Growing Interest, Emerging Perspectives. *Journal of the Academy of Marketing Science, 23*(4), 236-245.

Berry, L. L. (2002). Relationship Marketing of Services-Perspectives from 1983 and 2002. *Journal of Relationship Marketing, 1*(1), 59-77.

Boles, J. S., Babin, B. J., Brashear, T. G., & Brooks, C. (2001). An Examination of the Relationships between Retail Work Environments, Salesperson Selling Orientation-Customer Orientation and Job Performance. *Journal of Marketing Theory and Practice, 9*(3), 1-13.

Bone, P. F. (1992). Determinants of Word-of-Mouth Communications During Product Consumption. *Advances in Consumer Research, 19*, 579-583.

Chan, K. K., & Misra, S. (1990). Characteristics of the Opinion Leader: A New Dimension. *Journal of Advertising, 19*(3), 53-60.

Chaney, I. M. (2001). Opinion leaders as a segment for marketing communications. *Marketing Intelligence & Planning, 19*(5), 302-308.

Faison, E. W. J. (1977). The Neglected Variety Drive: A Useful Concept for Consumer Behavior. *Journal of Consumer Research, 4*, 172-175.

Gatignon, H., & Robertson, T. S. (1985). A Propositional Inventory for New Diffusion Research. *Journal of Consumer Research, 11*(4), 849-867.

Givon, M. (1984). Variety Seeking Through Brand Switching. *Marketing Science, 3*(1), 1-22.

Grönroos, C. (1990). Relationship Approach to Marketing in Service Contexts: The Marketing and Organizational Behavior Interface. *Journal of Business Research, 20*(1), 3-11.

Gummesson, E. (2001). Productivity, Quality and Relationship Marketing in Service Operations. In M. Bruhn & H. Meffert (Eds.), *Handbuch Dienstleistungsmanagement. Von der strategischen Konzeption zur praktischen Umsetzung* (Vol. 2, pp. 851-872). Wiesbaden: Gabler.

Heskett, J. L., Sasser, W. E., & Schlesinger, L. A. (1997). The Service Profit Chain. How Leading Companies Link Profit and Growth to Loyalty, Satisfaction, and Value. New York: The Free Press.

Heskett, J. L., Jones, T. O., Loveman, G. W., Sasser, W. E., & Schlesinger, L. A. (1994). Putting the Service-Profit Chain to Work. *Harvard Business Review, 72*, 164-174.

Hirschman, E. C., & Wallendorf, M. (1980). Some Implications of Variety Seeking for Advertising and Advertisers. *Journal of Advertising, 9*(2), 17-19, 43.

Hoyer, W. D., & Ridgway, N. M. (1984). Variety Seeking as an Explanation for Exploratory Purchase Behavior: A Theoretical Model. *Advances in Consumer Research, 11*, 114-119.

Jones, T. O., & Sasser, W. E. (1995). Why Satisfied Customers Defect. *Harvard Business Review, 73*, 88-99.

McAlister, L. (1982). A Dynamic Attribute Satiation Model of Variety-Seeking Behavior. *Journal of Consumer Research, 9*(2), 141-150.

McAlister, L., & Pessemier, E. A. (1982). Variety Seeking Behavior: An Interdisciplinary Review. *Journal of Consumer Research, 9*(3), 311-322.

Morgan, R. M., & Hunt, S. D. (1994). The Commitment-Trust Theory of Relationship Marketing. *Journal of Marketing, 58*(3), 20-38.

Myers, J. H., & Robertson, T. S. (1972). Dimensions of Opinion Leadership. *Journal of Marketing Research, 9*(1), 41-46.

Price, L. L., & Arnould, E. (1999). Commercial friendships: service provider-client relationships in context. *Journal of Marketing, 63*(4), 38-56.

Raju, P. S. (1980). Optimum Stimulation Level: Its Relationship to Personality, Demographics, and Exploratory Behavior. *Journal of Consumer Research, 7*(3), 272-282.

Ratner, R. K., & Kahn, B. E. (2002). The Impact of Private vs. Public Consumption on Variety-Seeking Behavior. *Journal of Consumer Research, 29*(2), 246-257.

Richins, M. L. (1983). Negative Word-of-Mouth by Dissatisfied Customers: A Pilot Study. *Journal of Marketing, 47*(1), 68-78.

Rust, R. T., Zahorik, A. J., & Keiningham, T. L. (1995). Return on quality (ROQ): Making Service Quality Financially Accountable. *Journal of Marketing, 59*(April), 58-70.

Summers, J. O. (1970). The Identity of Women's Clothing Fashion Opinion Leaders. *Journal of Marketing Research, 7*(2), 178-185.

Taylor, J. W. (1977). A Striking Characteristic of Innovators. *Journal of Marketing Research, 14*(1), 104-107.

van Trijp, H. C. M., Hoyer, W. D., & Inman, J. J. (1996). Why Switch? Product Category Level Explanations for True Variety Seeking Behavior. *Journal of Marketing Research, 33*(3), 281-292.

Woratschek, H., & Horbel, C. (2002). Managing Job Variety Seeking Behavior. In F. Bliemel, A. Eggert, & G. Fassott (Eds.), *Proceedings of the tenth International Colloquium in Relationship Marketing* (pp. 751-769). Kaiserslautern.

Zeithaml, V. A., Berry, L. L., & Parasuraman, A. (1996). The Behavioral Consequences of Service Quality. *Journal of Marketing, 60*(April), 31-46.

Zeithaml, V. A., & Bitner, M. J. (2000). *Services Marketing. Integrating Customer Focus Across the Firm* (2 ed.). Boston: Irwin McGraw-Hill.

The 4Ps of Relational Marketing, Perspectives, Perceptions, Paradoxes and Paradigms: Learnings from Organizational Theory and the Strategy Literature

Jaqueline Pels

Universidad Torcuato Di Tella, Argentina

Michael Saren

University of Strathclyde, Scotland

SUMMARY. The aim of this paper is to explore how different underlying worldviews in marketing affect the perception of the environment and how these impact the choice between transactional or relational offerings. Furthermore, we aim to show that not only positivistic and interpretivist paradigms are present in *all* of the management disciplines, in strategy, in organizational theory, in marketing, etc., but also that managerial disciplines seem to be moving from the reign of the positivistic schools, through the emergence of the interpretativist schools, and now towards a pluralistic approach.

Jaqueline Pels, PhD, is Professor of Marketing, Universidad Torcuato Di Tella, Miñones 2159, 1428 Capital Federal, Argentina (E-mail: jaquie@mail.retina.ar).

Michael Saren, PhD, is Professor of Marketing, University of Strathclyde, Cathedral Street 199, Glasgow, Scotland (E-mail: michael.saren@strath.ac.uk).

[Haworth co-indexing entry note]: "The 4Ps of Relational Marketing, Perspectives, Perceptions, Paradoxes and Paradigms: Learnings from Organizational Theory and the Strategy Literature." Pels, Jaqueline, and Michael Saren. Co-published simultaneously in *Journal of Relationship Marketing* (Best Business Books, an imprint of The Haworth Press, Inc.) Vol. 4, No. 3/4, 2005, pp. 59-84; and: *The Future of Relationship Marketing* (ed: David Bejou, and Adrian Palmer) Best Business Books, an imprint of The Haworth Press, Inc., 2005, pp. 59-84. Single or multiple copies of this article are available for a fee from The Haworth Document Delivery Service [1-800-HAWORTH, 9:00 a.m. - 5:00 p.m. (EST). E-mail address: docdelivery@haworthpress.com].

The analysis of the underlying worldviews is important for relationship marketing in practice because it may provide another, deeper-level explanation for the choices that managers make regarding transactional, relational and pluralistic offerings. At the theoretical level, it may help explain how and why the new RM paradigm developed in the marketing discipline. *[Article copies available for a fee from The Haworth Document Delivery Service: 1-800-HAWORTH. E-mail address: <docdelivery@haworthpress. com> Website: <http://www.HaworthPress.com> © 2005 by The Haworth Press, Inc. All rights reserved.]*

KEYWORDS. Research paradigms, theoretical paradigms in marketing

INTRODUCTION

If we interpret the development of marketing thought in Kuhnian terms (1970), then up until the 1980s marketing can be said to have had a single monolithic dominating approach: i.e., the transactional approach. Since the emergence of the relational approach there has been a strong debate on whether or not one of the two would dominate the other. That is, if relationships are an intensification of the transactional marketing (very much the US school) or, if on the other hand, transactions were episodes within relationships (associated with the European standing). More recently, a third position has started to emerge which argues that both paradigms will coexist (the Contemporary Marketing Practice-CMP-approach).

Our position is that the transactional approach (TM) and the relational approach (RM) are strongly influenced by two different underlying worldviews, with different assumptions, understandings and philosophical bases: the positivistic and the interpretative approaches respectively. Essentially the transactional approach believes that the organization creates value by understanding (through market research) the demand and responding with an adequate marketing mix, and it perceives the environment as external and objective and good marketing implies the survival of the fittest (i.e., that with the largest market share). On the other hand, the relational approach believes that value is co-created, through interaction with a network of actors: the customer, the supplier, the customer's customer and other stakeholders and, following the interpretativist logic, it perceives the environment and organization as mutually affecting each other.

The positivistic and the interpretative approaches to the organization-environment relationship are present in *all* of the management disciplines, in strategy, in organizational theory, in marketing, etc.

Bourgeois (1980, pp 25) states "Strategic decision making is at the heart of the organization-environment co-alignment process so heavily emphasized in both the business policy and organization theory literature. This co-alignment delineates the activities through which organizational leaders establish . . . how it will navigate or compete within its chosen domain(s)."

Mintzberg, Ahlstrand and Lampel (1998, pp 24) states, "Unexamined assumptions that appear perfectly plausible can sometimes prove to be rather misleading. We wish to raise doubts about these assumptions, not to dismiss the important contribution of the . . . school, but to understand better where it fits, alongside the very different views of some other schools". . . . Mintzberg (1998, pp 150) "Prior to the work of the cognitive school, what took place in the mind of managers was terra incognita."

We will seek to understand if the current coexistence of multiple schools is the consequence of a paradigmatic shift or other possible explanations. In other words, the present situation can be the result of:

- Either a paradigmatic shift (and the coexistence of multiple schools are just a symptom of the swing of the pendulum), or
- Is the rich center where knowledge should have always been. As Mintzberg, Ahlstrand and Lampel (1998, pp. 20) state "The field of strategic management may be moving towards a synthesis. As we shall see some of the newer work cut across our schools. . . . We applaud such work. It suggests a certain coming of age of the field."

The papers will start by discussing how the environment has been defined by the literature, next we'll be reviewing the organizational theory and the strategy literature to see how these disciplines have addressed the issue of the two paradigms and the environment-organization relationship, finally it will discuss the learnings from this literature review and its implications for the current debate in the field of marketing.

DEFINING THE ENVIRONMENT

On the Ontological Assumptions on the Environment

Bourgeois (1980) looks at the history of the discussion on holding an objective versus a subjective reading of the environment. Bourgeois states that Dill (1958) uses objective indicators, however Thompson

(1967, pp 159) promulgates that coping with uncertainty is the essence of the administrative process leading Weick to argue that it is only thought the managerial perceptions that the environment becomes 'known' to the organization and to the more radical position of Hambrick and Snow (1977, p 110) that state that the objective reality of physical environmental attributes is consequently 'less important' in determining or influencing organizational action. Finally, Bourgeois argues that reliance on perceived environment neglects the very concept of external environment and the constrains it places on the organization, the author wraps up declaring that "my position is that the objective task environment is 'real,' measurable, and external to the organization and that perceptions of the organizations are also real events taking place *within* the organization . . . crucial inputs to the strategy-making process."

Thus though Bourgeois recognizes that there is an objective and a perceived environment his description of the perceived environment is linked to the difficulties that managers' encounter in describing it (and thus assumes that there is an external objective environment) rather than a subjective composition of the environmental elements. On the other hand social constructionists argue that since the environments are within the organization they are little more than the product of managerial beliefs.

In 1985, Smircich and Stubbart go one step further and seek to answer the questions: Is the "environment" constructed? Is there no real objective environment? The authors (1985, pp. 725-726) describe three competing conceptions of the environment:

- The objective environment. . . . [This] assumes that an 'organization' is embedded within an 'environment' that has an external and independent existence. . . . Terms that seem to capture this sense of 'environment' include concrete, objective, independent, given, imminent, out there. . . . Nearly all strategic management research and writing incorporates this assumption . . . environment analysis thus entails discovery, or finding things that are *already somewhere* waiting to be found . . . [and then] to delineate a strategy that will meet [them].
- The perceived environment. . . . [This does not mean] a change in the conception of environment (which remains real, material, and external). Instead, the difference . . . involves a distinction about strategists. Strategists are permanently trapper by bounded rationality . . . and by their incomplete and imperfect perceptions of the 'environment'. . . . From a practical standpoint, the challenge . . . is

minimizing the gap between [their] flawed perceptions and the reality of their environment.

- The enacted environment. . . . From an interpretative worldview, *separate objective* 'environments' simply do not exist. . . . Instead, organizations and environments are convenient labels for patterns of activity. What people refer to as their environment is generated by human actions and accompanying intellectual efforts to make sense out of their actions. . . . The world is essentially and ambiguous field of experience. There are no threats or opportunities out there in the environment, just material and symbolic records of action. But a strategist–determined to find meaning-makes relationships by bringing connections and patterns to action. . . . Strategist create imaginary lines between events, objects, and situations so that [they] become meaningful for the members of an organizational world.

More recently, Oswald et al. (1997) state that "despite attempts to objectively gather and process pertinent information, industry and competition evaluations are likely to include varying degrees of subjective judgment from managers who are processing the information. That is, although environmental analyses (both internal and external) may have objective aims, research suggests that the interpretation of these analyses is influenced by the individual judgments and perceptions of the involved managers (Bourgeois, 1985; Daft & Weick, 1984; Smircich & Stubbart, 1985)."

EPISTEMOLOGICAL POSITIONS IN THE ORGANIZATIONAL THEORY AND STRATEGY LITERATURE

In this section we address the epistemological positions in organizational theory and the strategy literature. First, we briefly discuss the importance of a given epistemological position in decision-making. Next, we review the organizational and strategy schools that hold a positivistic perspective. We close the section with a discussion of the schools that have grown out of the interpretativistic approach.

Shrivastava and Mitroff (1984) highlight the importance of assumptions in organizational decision-making. They argue that assumptions lead to sustain certain selective views of reality (Argyris and Schon,

1978; Mitroff and Emshoff, 1979) and are the underlying ground of organizational reality.

Furthermore, Shrivastava and Mitroff (1984) remind us that managers selectively choose, from the jungle of existing theories, those that most closely describe their own world views and ideologies (Dunbar, Dutton and Torbert, 1982; Starbuck, 1982). Managers use theories and knowledge claims that are consistent with their own frame of reference (Thomas and Tymon, 1982, Weiss and Bucuvalas, 1908).

Part of this section draws heavily on Gareth Morgan's book 'Images of Organization' (1986). Thus, before moving forwards, we need to understand what are Morgan's assumptions about the nature of reality and knowledge. Morgan believes in a position that attempts to recognize the paradox that reality is simultaneously subjective and objective. He states that "we *engage* objective realities subjectively: by putting ourselves into what we 'see', in a way that actually influences what we see. The process can be understood as one of 'engagement' and 'co-production', involving both subjective constructions and concrete interactions between real 'others'"(pp 382).

In his book Morgan (Chapter 1) invites us to read a situation from 'new angles', using different metaphors to interpret a given situation. Morgan defines metaphors as "theories or conceptual frameworks" (pp 336) . . . "Metaphor implies a *way of thinking and a way of seeing* that pervade how we understand our world generally" (pp 12) and warns us not to fall in love with a given perspective as metaphors highlight certain interpretations and tend to force others into a background role. As a matter of fact, Morgan believes that an effective analysis rests in being able to take account of rival theories. Furthermore, he states that to achieve a comprehensive 'reading' we need to see how these different aspects may coexist in a complementary or even paradoxical way. In other words, he invites us to be open and integrative of the different approaches.

We appreciate Morgan's insight on the value of metaphors but wish to distance ourselves in terms of the application we'd like to do of them.

First, Morgan stresses the importance of using multiple metaphors in order to achieve an enriched picture of organizations. On the other hand, we are interested in the fact that different metaphor highlight particular perspectives and that organizations, due to their culture and assumptions, normally adopt *a* given metaphor.

Second, Morgan tries to encourage *change*, inviting the reader to depart from a monolithic perspective towards a pluralistic approach while we want to take *a picture of the dominating metaphor* (with regards to the organization/environment relation) and see how it impacts the choice of a given offer proposition.

Having clarified our position with regards to these two aspects it is still necessary to specify that not all the organizational theory approaches have dealt with or focused their attention on our topic of interest: the environment-organization relationship. Having clarified these limitations let's look at the epistemological approaches that seem to emerge from the literature review.

A POSITIVIST APPROACH
IN ORGANIZATIONAL THEORY AND STRATEGY

The Positivist Schools Within Organizational Theory:[1]
The Environment as External and Objective and the Survival of the Fittest

Three of Morgan's (1986) metaphors, the contingency theory, the population ecology, and the information-processing systems assume the environment as external and given, and that organizations need to choose the organizational structure that will allow the best adaptation to it. As stated before, Morgan's book does not have as its focus the organization-environment relation though in discussing the metaphors it addresses the issue. In this subsection I will briefly introduce the three metaphors and simultaneously bring in articles that address the environment-organization topic from the perspective of each metaphor.

The open system approach, which includes the *contingency theory* and the *population-ecology view of organizations*, introduce and highlight the role of the environment. This is a very significant contribution, however, it is important to understand exactly what was meant by environment and how the relation between organization and environment is described. First, the environment is considered as given and researchers are centred in understanding changes, uncertainties, and dynamics of the environment. Second, though there is a genuine shift in the focus from efficiency towards effectiveness, effectiveness is seen as adaptation for survival to a given environment. The contingency theory ultimate aim is to help organizations reach a 'good fit' in order to be better able to survive *than other organizations* (thus the focus is on resource scarcity, competition, and survival of the fittest). However, the contingency approach recognises that in some cases a good fit is the classical bureaucratic organization and, in other cases, the organic organization

(Burns & Stalker 1950s). Third, these schools look at the link between environment and strategy, but strategy is seen as the choice of the correct organizational structure that allows a correct adaptation to the environment. In this discussion of the environment there is no distinction between the Macro (general context) and the Micro (task environment).

The academics studying organizations as *information-processing systems* are also interested in the organization-environment relation. Here, the focus is set on how to overcome the issues of bounded rationality, especially when dealing with complexity and environmental uncertainty. Different solutions are suggested: reducing information needs, increasing information processing capacity, and/or developing learning abilities. The whole idea of environmental uncertainty is implicitly linked to the difficulty of reaching 'full knowledge' and how to minimize the risks derived from imperfect know-how. The aim is to understand a 'given yet changing environment.' Down deep the classical decision-making model of seeking the 'optimum' (probably a dynamical optimum) is perceived as the ideal to achieve and all the other strategies and processes are 'just second best'. In other words, the idea of an objective environment still governs the thinking of these scholars.

The Positivist Schools Within Strategy: Strategy as the Match Between the External and Objective Environment and the Organizational Resources and Capabilities

It is interesting to notice that a great majority of the models presented in the strategy literature state that the environment is external to the organization. Though many authors accept that the environment can be subjectively perceived this subjectivity is normally seen as the result of managerial biases or limitations due to bounded rationality, scarcity of information, scanning methodology and/or similar constraints that lead to diverse degrees of environmental myopia. Chaffee (1985), Hart (1992) and Mintzberg, Ahlstrand and Lampel (1998) propose different classifications of strategy school. None of them take the organization-environment as their main classification criteria, however it is discussed in the description of the schools. We shall give a concise description of the three classifications and the positivist schools discussed by them.

Chaffee (1985) highlights the importance of the organization-environment relationship. She states, "A basic premise of thinking about strategy concerns the inseparability of organizations and environment . . . the organization uses strategy to deal with changing environments." Chaffee identifies three mental models representing three distinct and, in some ways, conflicting views on strategy: the linear, the adaptive and the interpretative. The first two assume that the organization-environment boundaries are permeable:

Linear strategy, 'Strategy is the determination of basic long-term goals of an enterprise and the adoption of courses of action and the allocation of resources necessary for carrying out these goals. (Chandler 1962, pp 13)' In other words, strategy planning, formulation, and implantation.

The environment is assumed to be 'out there' and composed mainly of competitors and it is assumed that it is either predictable (so that the changes that occur between the planning stage and the implantation phase can be contemplated in the planning stage) or else the organization is well insulated from the environment.

Adaptive strategy, 'Strategy concerned with the development of a viable match between the opportunities and risks present in the external environment and the organization's capabilities and resources for exploiting these opportunities' (Hofer, 1973, pp3). This model seeks a permanent assessment of the environment and the organization in order to achieve a perfect and continuous match between the two.

This model assumes that the organization-environment boundaries are permeable (this model relies heavily on the biological model of organizational theory). The environment is seen as more dynamic and less predictable and the organization is assumed to have to change *with* the changing environment.

Hart (1992) proposes an integrative framework for strategy-making process consisting of five models: command, symbolic, rational, transactive, and generative. The framework is based on the varying roles top managers and organizational members play in the strategy-making process. Before discussing his categorization Hart summarizes the historical evolution of the field identifying different schools of thought.

The *rational* model (Meyerson and Banfield, 1955) which implies that decision makers consider all available alternatives, identify and evaluate all the consequences, and select the alternative that would be preferable in terms of the most valued ends. The rational model applied to strategy suggests a systematic environmental analysis and is embedded in the strong assumption that the environment is external to the organization and that it is the source of opportunities and/or threats.

The *behavioral theory* (Cyert and March, 1963) challenges the assumptions of rationality and develops around the core concept of bounded rationality (Simon, 1957). Though academics now accept that managers rely in cognitive maps to organize issues and events into manageable sets of categories and depart from the concept of optimality, this does not mean that these authors depart from the idea that there is an external objective environment, they are just stating that is difficult to know it in a way that allows a perfectly rational decision.

The *muddling through* (Lindblom, 1959) and *garbage can* models of strategic choice result from political conflicts in organizations. Here the focus moves from looking at the environment and trying to understand it (totally or partially) to studying how the organization and its internal limitations affect and condition the strategy making process. Quinn (1978) proposed *logical incrementalism* as the normative ideal for strategy making. In this model top managers may be able to predict the broad direction but not the precise nature of the ultimate strategy that will result. Thus, rather than seeking to be comprehensive–the ideal of rationality–top managers work to create a general sense of purpose and direction that will guide the actions taken by organizational members. Though Quinn clearly distinguishes logical incrementalism form muddling through, from an organization-environment relation, in all three models the focus moves from looking at the environment and trying to understand it (totally or partially) to studying how the organization and its internal limitations affect and condition the strategy making process.

Mintzberg, Ahlstrand and Lampel (1998) classify three schools within this approach, the design school, the planning school and the positioning school.

The Design school represents, without question, the most influential view of the strategy-formation process. Its key concepts continue to form the base of undergraduate and MBA strategy courses. At its simplest, the design school proposes a model of strategy making that seeks to attain a match, or fit, between internal capabilities and external possibilities. Its Origins: Selznick (1957-Berkley) introduces the concept of 'distinctive competence' and the need to bring together internal state with external expectations; Chandler (1962-MIT) established the notion of business strategy and its relations to organizational structure; Rumelt (1997) argues that, after analysis, top management must choose between *several alternative* strategies and choose the best one.

The planning School's central message is about formal procedures, formal training, and formal analysis. It originated with Ansoff, 1965. Several strategic planning models emerged (i.e., SWOT) each divided into neat steps with objectives up-front and budgets and operating plans on the back end.

The positioning school adds content to the prescriptive outlook of the design and planning schools. The watershed year was 1980 with Porter's book Competitive Strategy. Porter took its lead from the economic school of industrial organization.[2] In contrast to the design and planning school the positioning school argued that only a few key strategies are desirable in a given industry (vis-à-vis unique company-specific strategies), thus developing 3 *generic* strategies. Thus the focus was on identifying the right fit between predefined generic industry characteristics (i.e., fragmented-concentrated) and one of the three generic strategies. Thus the concept of strategy preceding structure (from the design and planning schools) is retained, but a new form of structure (the industry structure) was added on top. Furthermore Porter introduced a whole new set of concepts (i.e., new entrants, value chain, strategic groups, etc.). It is within this school that the BCG growth-share matrix, the experience curves, and the PIMS databases flourish. More recently strategy researchers from this school have also drawn on another popular field in economics: game theory.

AN INTERPRETATIVIST APPROACH
IN ORGANIZATIONAL THEORY AND STRATEGY

Following a chronological order, We shall introduce authors that have specialized in different managerial disciplines and belong to different schools of thought within their field yet share a communality: they all take an interpretativist approach to their topic of study. We dare say that these are the founding fathers (and mothers) of the interpretativist approach in management. After the presentation of the key thinkers of this paradigm We shall briefly develop the main interpretativist schools within Organizational Theory and Strategy.

Founding Fathers (and Mothers) of the Interpretativist Approach in Management

Selznick (1957, in Mintzberg 1987) wrote about *the 'character' of an organization–distinct and integrated 'commitments to ways of acting and responding' that are built right into it.* A variety of concepts from other fields also capture this notion:

- Psychologists refer to an individual's mental frame, cognitive structure, and a variety of other expressions for 'relatively fixed patterns for experiencing [the] world' (Bieri, 1971).
- Anthropologists refer to the 'culture' of a society.
- Sociologists to its 'ideology'.
- Behavioral scientists, who have read Kuhn (1970) on the philosophy of science, refer to the 'paradigm' of a community of scholars.

Germans perhaps capture it best with their word 'Weltanschauung', literally 'worldview,' meaning collective intuition about how the world works.

On discussing interpretations Weick (1979, pp171-175,-in Weick and Daft, 1983, pp75) states, " it is plausible to portray organizations as embedded in an environment of puns" and "interpretations interpret interpretations rather than events." The idea behind these statements is that there is no univocal reading; rather there are multiple possible 'correct' alternative interpretations of events. Interpretation is the process through which information is given meaning and actions are chosen (Daft and Weick, 1984). In their 1983 work Weick and Daft develop a model of organizations as interpretative systems and distinguish between organizations that assume that the environment is objective and those that assume that it is subjective. In the latter case the interpretation shapes the environment more than the environment shapes the interpretation.

Mintzberg (1987) in his debate of the strategy concept discusses the definition of strategy as a *perspective*. Mintzberg argues, "This definition of strategy looks inside the organization, indeed inside the heads of the collective strategist. Here, *strategy is a perspective*, its content consisting not just of a chosen position, but of an ingrained way of perceiving the world. What is of key importance about this definition, however, is that the perspective is *shared*. As implied in the words Weltanschauung, culture, and ideology (with respect to a society) or paradigm (with respect to a community of scholars), but not the word personality, strategy is a perspective shared by the members of an organization, through their intentions and/or actions.

The Interpretative Schools Within Organizational Theory[3]

Four of Morgan's (1986) metaphors reinforce the idea of diversity in the manager's perception. First the organizational ecology approach sees environments as negotiated environments rather that independent external forces. Then, culture metaphor develops the topic of firms (specifically managers within the firms) as sense-makers, next, the flux metaphor is discussed as it calls our attention towards the underlying logics and assumptions in the development of a worldview, and finally the psychic prison metaphor is introduced as it debates the resulting risks of myopia related to any organization with a strong monolithic approach.

The population-ecology and contingency views perceive organizations as existing in a state of tension or struggle with their environment. Both presume that organization and environment are separate phenomena. Under *modern system theory*, however, this kind of assumption has attracted increasing criticism. For organizations are not discrete entities, even though it may be convenient to think of them as such. Many biologists now believe that it is the whole ecosystem that evolves, and the process of evolution can really be understood only at the level of total ecology. This has important implications, it suggests that evolution is always evolution of a pattern of relations embracing organisms *and* their environment. It is the *pattern*, not just the separate units comprising this pattern that evolves.

The *organizational ecology approach* picks up these ideas and introduces the concept of the survivals of the fitting, not just the fittest (Boulding, 1956). Boulding states that organizations and their environments are engaged in a pattern of co-creation, where each produces the other. Environments then become in some measure always negotiated environments, rather than independent external forces. The ecological perspective makes two important contributions. First, organizational environments can be seen as being a product of human creativity, in other words they can be understood as socially constructed phenomena. Second, resources can be abundant and self-renewing and that organisms collaborate as well as compete and thus distinguishes itself from the evolution approach that emphasizes the survival of the fittest encouraging competition as the basic rule of organizational life. Managers in organizations that perceive the environment and the organization as belonging to an eco-system concentrate on issues of fitting, focusing on cooperation rather than competition between actors.

The Organizations as Cultures. The organizations as cultures approach, focuses on organizations as socially constructed realities (pp. 112). In talking about culture we are really talking about a process of reality construction that allows people to see and understand particular events, actions, objects, utterances, or situations in distinctive ways (pp. 128). Hence organizations rest in shared systems of meaning and shared interpretative schemes. Organizational psychologist Karl Weick has described the process through which we shape and structure our realities as a process of *enactment*. Weick's concept stresses the proactive role that we unconsciously play in creating our world through various interpretative schemes (pp. 130).

Though this approach is mainly centered on the culture-organization axis (culture as the 'normative glue') it can also help us reinterpret the nature and significance of the organization-environment relations (pp. 136-7). We can understand the way an organization makes sense of its environment as a process of social enactment. Organizations choose and structure their environment through a host of interpretive decisions. One's knowledge of (and relations with) the environment are extensions of one's culture (pp. 136-7), since we come to know and understand our environment through the belief systems that guide our interpretations and actions. Environmental turbulence and change is a product of this ongoing process of enactment.[4] Environments are enacted by hosts of organizations each acting on the basis of their interpretations of a world that is in effect mutually defined. A competitive ethos produces competitive environments.

This has profound implications for how we understand organization-environment relations and strategic management (pp. 136-7). We choose and operate in environmental domains according to how we construct conceptions of what we are and what we are trying to do. By appreciating that strategy making is a process of enactment that produces a large element of the future with which the organization will have to deal, it is possible to overcome the false impression that organizations are adapting or reacting to a world that is independent of their own making.

The Flux Metaphor. Organizations can also be seen from the logics involved in the change process. Bohm (a theoretical physicist) argues that the state of the universe at any point is time reflects a more basic reality (the *implicated* order) to be distinguished from the *explicated* order. The explicated order permitted a degree of autonomy but is always dependent on deeper forces within the implicated order. In essence, there is a search for an explanation of the deep structure of social life, of the logics of change. Understanding a problem in terms of the logics of change that produce it opens many different scenarios, often involving possible change on the logic of the system itself. Often this will lead to a new understanding of the interests represented in the problem, and a reformulation of the relations between those involved (pp. 269-70). Morgan suggests three sources (additional to the unconscious and culture): autopoiesis, circular relations, and dialectic relations.

Autopoiesis[5] (Maturana and Varela) challenges the validity of the distinction drawn between system and environment. Maturana and Varela believe that living systems are closed and autonomous, that they are a closed loop of interactions. They accept that we can make entities distinct but argue that this process is arbitrary and artificial. Maturana and Varela also have strong reservation about the application of their theory to the social world, however, Morgan invites us to use the core ideas the autopoiesis approach puts forward.

First, when discussing organizations as cultures we gave attention to the idea that organizations enact their environments, in other words, they assign patterns of variation and significance to the world in which they operate. The ideas of autopoiesis encourage us to view organizational enactment as part of the self-referential process. In other terms, the figures, mkt trends, competitive position, sales forecasts, and so forth (in Bohm's terms the explicated order) are really projections of the organization's own interests and concerns. They reflect the organization's understanding of itself (in Bohm's terms the implicated order). It is through this process of self-reference that organizational members can intervene in their own functioning.

Second, Many of the problems organizations encounter when dealing with their environments are intimately connected with the kind of identity that they try to maintain. Many organizations are preoccupied with understanding their environment as a kind of 'world out there' that has an existence of its own. These firms see the environment as creating opportunities or threats and their task is to survive. These organizations draw boundaries around narrow definitions of themselves. On the other hand, autopoiesis help firms recognize that the environment is not an independent domain and that it isn't necessary to struggle against it, thus allowing for a new type of relations to be established between organization and environment.

The mutual causality perspective encourages us to think about change in terms of loops rather than lines. The logic of such systems rests in the network of *relations* that define and sustain patterns of causality.

The Organization as Psychic Prisons. The organization as psychic prisons metaphor encourages managers to recognize the importance of probing the strength and weaknesses of the assumptions that shape how the organizations view and deal with their world. The metaphor encourages us to understand that while organizations may be socially constructed realities, these constructions create ways of seeing and acting, but also create ways of not seeing, and eliminate the possibility of actions associated with alternative views of the world, thus preventing them form dealing with their environment in an effective manner. This approach acts as a counter balance that invites us to caution and probe if our social construction is sound and not the result of unconscious processes and related patterns of control that trap people in unsatisfactory modes of existence.

In organization theory the idea of challenging taken-for-granted ways of thinking is becoming well established, especially in work of theorists recognizing the role of paradigms and metaphors in shaping how we think (e.g., Burrell and Morgan, 1979; Morgan 1980; Schon, 1963, 1979). At a practical level this has developed into the ideas that problems solutions (-yo-decisions) depend on the way problems are framed, and that we can develop methodologies to escape cognitive traps by engaging in dialectic and other modes of critical thinking (e.g., Mason and Mitroff, 1981).

The Interpretative Schools Within Strategy[6]

Different authors have sought to categorize the existing literature on strategy (i.e., Chaffee, 1985; Hart, 1992; Mintzberg, Ahlstrand and Lampel, 1998), unfortunately, none of the quoted authors has taken the organization-environment relation as the key categorization variable. However, these classifications have either declared explicit standings or have clear assumptions about the organization-environment relation.

In the positivist approach section we have discussed Chaffee's (1985) linear and adaptive strategies, here we shall discuss the *Interpretative strategy* model. Chaffee argues that this approach parallels recent works in corporate culture and symbolic management outside the strategy literature (OT authors: Pfeffer, 1981, Smircich and Morgan, 1982, Weick and Daft, 1983). This model assumes that reality is socially constructed (book: Berger and Luckmann, 1966). That is, that reality is not something objective or external to the perceiver that can be apprehended correctly or incorrectly. Rather reality is defined through a process of social interchange in which perceptions are affirmed, modified, or replaced according to their apparent congruence with the perceptions of others. Strategy in the interpretative model might be defined as orienting metaphors or frames of reference that allow the organization and its environment to be understood by organizational stakeholders. Hatten (1979, book) envisaged a new theory of strategy that was oriented towards managerial perceptions, conflict and consensus.

From his literature review, Hart (1992) identifies three recurring themes related to the strategy-making process: rationality, vision and involvement. Of the three, vision is the one that relate to this section. Hart doesn't really define a position of its own, but rather quotes the works of colleagues he believe have worked from this approach though using different names, such as, Chaffee's (1985) *interpretative* model, Mintzberg's (1987) *perspective* mode, and Bourgeois and Brodwin's (1984) *cultural* mode. All reflect the subjective aspect of the strategy-making process and are concerned with identifying the metaphors and frames of reference that allow organizational stakeholders to understand the organization and its environment.

Mintzberg, Ahlstrand and Lampel (1998) see the cognitive school as the bridge between the more objective schools: design, planning and positioning, and the more subjective schools: learning, power, culture, environment and configuration. The cognitive school focuses on studying the mind of the strategist and the mental structures it has to organize knowledge; the learning school sees strategies as emerging as people, mostly acting collectively, come to learn about a situation as well as their organization's capability of dealing with it. The power school sees strategy as shaped by power and politics. The culture school brings the interpretative wing of the cognitive school to life in the collective world of organizations. The configuration school seeks to reconciliate and integrate all the previous schools.

The Cognitive School, Strategy as a Mental Process. More than a tight school of thought this body of work is a loose collection of research though it is growing into a more robust school. Their focus is studying the mind of the strategist and the mental structures it has to organize knowledge. *There are two 'wings':*

- The *positivistic*, that looks outwards and seeks to produce some kind of objective picture of the world, though it acknowledges several biases, distortions and limitations. In other words, it tries to re-create the world.
- The *subjective*, that looks inwards and tries to understand how the mind interprets the world. In other words, it tries to create the world. Cognition as *construction views strategy* as interpretation (pp. 164-171).[7] To the proponents of this view, the world "out there" does not simply drive behaviour "in here," even if through filters of distortion, bias, and simplification. There is more to cognition that some kind of effort to mirror reality. These people ask: What about the strategies that change the world? For the interpretative or constructionist view, what is inside the human mind is not a reproduction of the external world. *All that information flowing*

in through those filters, supposedly to be decoded by those cognitive maps, in fact *interacts with cognition and is shaped by it*. The mind, imposes some interpretation to the environment, it constructs the world. This view has radical implications. Researchers who subscribe to it, social constructionists, break decisively with the pervasive tendency to accept the world as give. To them, reality exists in our head. Under the constructionist perspective, *metaphors* become important as do symbolic actions and communications (Chaffee, 1985:94), *vision* emerges as more than an instrument for guidance: it becomes the leader's interpretation of the world made into a collective reality.

The Learning School, Strategy Formation as an Emergent Process. According to this school, strategies emerge as people, mostly acting collectively, come to learn about a situation as well as their organization's capability of dealing with it. This school questioned the basic assumptions of the 'rational' traditions of the design, planning and positioning school: who really is the architect of strategy? Where in the organization does strategy formation really take place? Is the separation between formulation and implementation really sacrosanct?

Lindblom's (1959) talks of disjointed incrementalism in strategy formulation providing the step-stone for Quinn's (1980) logical incrementalism which sees top management as trying to maintain a consistent pattern of what emerges from the decisions taken in the different sub-systems. Later Mintzberg and the McGill faculty of management distinguish between 'deliberate' (planned and based on control) and 'emergent' (action and learning based) strategy. Weick (1979) (Mintzberg, pp. 195-201) also contributes to this school when he states that *management is inextricably bound up with the process of imposing sense on past experience*, thus breaking with decades of tradition which stated that 'thinking must end' before 'action begins' (that is, formulation precedes implementation). Furthermore, Weick based on the ecology model introduces the concept of enactment, selection (of what works), and retention (make sense of those actions that worked).

The Power School, Strategy as a Process of Negotiation. According to this school strategy is shaped by power and politics, whether as a process inside the organization (micro-power) or as the behaviour of the organization itself in its external environment (macro-power). Strategy from this perspective means managing the demands of these actors (suppliers, competitors, buyer unions, investment banks, etc.) and of selectively making use of them for the organizations benefits. In Pfeffer and Salancik's (1978) terms, "organizations adapt and change to fit the environmental requirements or . . . can attempt to alter the environment so that it fits [their] capabilities" (P&S: pp. 160).

Networks (IMP), *collective strategy* (collaboration over competition), *strategic alliances* (non-equity forms of cooperative agreements, usually between suppliers and customers), *joint ventures* (cooperative agreements with equity positions in new businesses), and *strategic sourcing* (outsourcing) have been called the 'boundary school' (Elfring and Volberda (1998), where *the negotiated aspects are central*. All of these approaches make it more difficult to define where one organization ends and another begins.

The Cultural School, Strategy as a Collective Cognition Process. Culture is essentially composed of interpretations of the world and the activities and artefacts that reflect these. Thus for this school, strategy formation is a process of social interaction, based on the beliefs and understandings shared by the members of an organization.

The cultural school brings the interpretative wing of the cognitive school to life in the collective world of organizations. As a result, organizations with different cultures operating in the same environment will interpret that environment in quite different ways. As noted in the cognitive school, they will see those things they want to see. An organization develops a 'dominant logic' that acts as an information filter, leading to a focus on some data for strategy making while ignoring others (Prahalad and Bettis, 1986).

Wernerfelt (1984), based on Penrose's studies, develops the *resource-based theory*. This 'inside-out' view (which is opposed to the positioning school's 'outside-in' view) focuses in internal capabilities and dynamic capabilities (Prahalad and Hamel). Resources are strategic if they are valuable, rare, inimitable and difficult to substitute, thus certain cultures can become a seen as a strategic resource.

The Environment School, Strategy as a Reactive Process. This school helps bring the overall view of strategy formation into balance, by positioning the *environment*, next to *organization* and *leadership*, as one of the central forces of the strategy formation process. Of course, 'environment' has not been absent from the other schools, but it was present in specific ways: in the *positioning* school, as a set of economic forces: competition, industry and market; in the interpretative wing of the *cognitive* school, as a place that sends out confusing signals, to complex to be fully understood; in the *learning* school, as a place to experiment with, and enact as well as learn from; in the other schools (design, planning, entrepreneurial, power and culture) the environment seems to be absent, incidental or assumed being the focus of strategy formation centred on the leader or the organization. In all the previous schools the strategist reigned supreme in this school the environment takes command.

The environmental school grows out of the *contingency theory*, here the belief was that there is 'one best way' to run an organization, thus a clear systematic description of the environment was necessary. Later the *population ecology* view introduce the variation-selection-retention model believing that there isn't much space to adapt to the environment through strategic choices as many basic structural aspects are fixed and act as strong constrains. Organizations that meet the environment's criteria of fit survive and those that do not are selected out. Lastly, the *institutional theorists* argue that the political and ideological pressures exerted by the environment reduce, but do not eliminate, strategic *choice*. All three schools allow a very restricted view to strategic choice with a strong predominance of the environment's *conditioning*.

On the other hand in the 'critique' section of this school Mintzberg et al. introduce a series of questions (pp. 297) But, if the environmental imperative is really so strong, how is it that two organizations can operate successfully in a similar environment with very different strategies? How distinct really is an organization from its 'environment', especially with the growth of alliances and joint ventures that blur the boundaries? Do environments 'select' organizations, or do organizations 'enact' environments? What is an 'industry environment' but all the organizations functioning in it? Moreover, do environments 'exist' at all, or are these just the perception of people-social constructions themselves?

The Configuration School, Strategy Formation as a Process of Transformation. This school seeks to reconciliate and integrate all the previous schools. There are two sides to this school: (1) one describes states–of the organizations and its surroundings–as *configurations*; (2) the other describes strategy making as *transformations*. These are two sides of the same coin: if an organization adopts states of being, then strategy making becomes the process of leaping from one state to another.

Configuration theorists see the world in nice, neat categories (outliers are ignored in favour of central tendencies). The key to strategic management is to sustain stability most of the time (adapting to a given configuration), but periodically to recognize the need for transformation (i.e., from start-up to a more formalized structure under professional management) and to manage that disruptive process without destroying the organization. Thus for this school all of the previous schools represent a particular configuration! Miller developed what he calls archetypes, which combine states of strategy, structure, situation, and process (1982, 1983, 1986). Smiles and Snow (1978) offer another categorization of corporate behaviour, combining strategy, technology, structure and process: defenders, prospectors, analysers and reactors.

Transformation, Miller and Friesen (1980b, 1982a, 1984) describe change in an organization as quantum, and call it strategic revolution, in contrast to gradual change. At these times, the organization tries to leap to a new stability to re-establish as quickly as possible an integrated posture among a new set of strategies, structure, and culture–in other words, a new configuration. Mintzberg presents the change cube that is about changing strategy and structure, ranging from conceptual to concrete and from formal to informal. Mintzberg (1997) also suggests a map where the methods of change are plotted on two dimensions, one representing macro-micro changes and the other three basic approaches to the process of change: planned change (or programmed), driven change (or guided), and evolved change (or organic).

CONCLUSIONS

Strategy, organizational theory and, now, marketing seem to be moving from the reign of the positivistic schools, which dictated that organizations needed to adapt to the environment, to the emergence of the interpretativist schools, which argue that reality is a social construction, towards a pluralistic approach, which accepts the co-existence of multiple, apparently contradictory, approaches.

Both Morgan (1986) and Mintzberg et al. (1998) have made a strong call in favor of using multiple metaphors or approaches as they see each school as over-emphasizing a particular aspect of the strategy process or organizational life. Both agree that each school, by focusing on a given aspect, has contributed to calling academics and managers' attention to that specific topic (i.e., the role of power), yet, simultaneously, each school has the downside of being biased. Thus the ideal seems to be a wide-ranging pluralistic approach, in Mintzberg's et al. words "ingredients of a stew" and in Morgan's terms "an effective analysis . . . takes into account rival theories . . . to achieve a comprehensive 'reading'."

This integrative effort is enriching as it calls our attention to issues, such as the role of the leader, of power, or of culture, that if ignored, might lead to a partial analyses. However, some of the schools discussed, rather than focusing in a particular topic, introduce a different ontological position. As a consequence, some schools present incommensurable differences. The big question no one seems to have answered is: can opposite perspectives coexist in one organization?

The configuration school links the schools by associating configurations to stages and accepts that change often comes in the form of quantum leaps or revolutionary shifts rather than an incremental process (Miller and Freisen 1980, 1982, 1984, in Mintzberg et al., pp. 313-4). In other words, at these times, the organization tries to leap to a new stability to re-establish as quickly as possible an integrated posture among a new set of strategies, structure, and culture, in other words, a new configuration. This seems to imply that a given organization can, in different moments of its life, assume different configurations and that the pluralism one perceives is the result of the configurations different firms have at a given point in time.

The literature review shows us that it could be very interesting to integrate our marketing studies with the work of our colleagues in the organization and strategy, and that the questions we are asking ourselves are not very distant from theirs. Thus, similarly to the interpretative schools in organizational theory and strategy, relationship marketing has brought new a perspective, new perceptions, in short, a new paradigm. This is important for relationship marketing in practice because it may provide another, deeper-level explanation for the possibilities, constraints and choices that managers make regarding transactional, relational and pluralistic offerings. At the theoretical level, it may help explain how and why the new RM paradigm developed in the marketing discipline.

There still remain a number of paradoxes for researchers in RM. (1) How can multiple paradigms coexist in the same firm? (2) How can firms address the same industry and market from different approaches and still be equally successful?

NOTES

1. This section draws heavily on Morgan's book, *Images of Organization*, 1986.

2. The theory of *industrial organizations* reflects the traditional economic-related view of the exchange environment. In this theory, the environment is seen as transparent and objective. Emphasis is placed on describing the structure of the environment through the number and type of firms operating in an industry (Wilson and Moller, 1995).

3. This section draws heavily on Morgan's book, *Images of Organization*, 1986.

4. useful discussion on the enactment of organizational culture can be found in Louise (1983) and Smircich (1983a). Huff (1982) and Smircich and Stubbart (1985)

show how organizations enact their environments. For details on the references see Gareth Morgan's book.

5. Morgan's 1982 work on corporate Strategy presents an approach that has much in common with the autopoietic viewpoint (pp. 373).

6. This section draws heavily on Mintzberg, Ahlstrand and Lampel, *Strategy Safari*, 1998

7. Chaffee (1985) placed the' interpretative' school along side with the 'rational view (our first three schools) and the 'adaptive' view (our learning school) as one of the three major approaches to strategy formation. Johnson (1987: 56-57) links the two main wings of the cognitive school with that of the 'cultural' school.

REFERENCES

Ansoff, H. I., "Corporate Strategy," New York: Mc. Graw-Hill, 1965.

Argyris, C. and Schon, D. A. "Organizational learning: A theory of action perspective." Reading MA: Addison-Wesley, 1978.

Berger, P. and Luckmann, T., "The social construction of reality." New York: Doubleday, 1966.

Bieri, J., "Cognitive Structure in Personality," in H.M. Schroder and P. Suedfeld, eds., *Personality: Theory and Information Processing*, New York, NY: Ronald Press, p. 178. By the same token, Bieri (p. 179) uses the word "strategy" in the context of psychology, 1971.

Bohm, D. "The Implicate Order: A New Order for Physics," Process Studies, 8: 73-102, 1978.

Boulding, K. E. "General Systems Theory–The Skeleton of Science." Management Science, 2: 197-208, 1956b.

Bourgeois, L. J, III "Strategy and Environment: A Conceptual Integration," Academy of Management Review, Vol. 5, No. 1, 25-39, 1980.

Bourgeois, L. J., III and Brodwin, David R. "Strategic Implementation: Five Approaches to an Elusive Phenomenon," Strategic Management Journal, Jul/Sep, Vol 5/3, 1984.

Bourgeois, L. J., "Strategic goals, perceived uncertainty, and economic performance in volatile environments," Academy of Management Journal, 28, 548-573, 1985.

Burrell, G. and G. Morgan. "Sociological Paradigms and Organizational Analysis." London: Heinemann Educational Books, 1979.

Chaffee, E. E., "Three Models of Strategy," Academy of Management Review, 10, 1: 89-98, 1985.

Chandler, A. D., Jr. "Strategy and Structure: Chapters in the History of the Industrial Enterprise," Cambridge, MA: MIT Press, 1962.

Cyert, R. and March J. "A behavioral theory of the firm." New York, Prentice Hall, 1963.

Daft, R. L., "Toward a model of organizations as interpretation systems," Academy of Management Review, 9 (2), 284-295, 1984.

Daft, R. L., Sormunen, J, and Parks, D., "Chief Executive Scanning, Environmental Characteristics and Company Performance: An Empirical Study," Strategic Management Journal, Vol. 9, 123-139, 1988.

Dill, W. R. "Environment as an influence on managerial autonomy," Administrative Science Quarterly, 2, 409-443, 1958.

Dunbar, R. L. M., Dutton, J. m and Torbert, W. R. "Crossing mother: Ideological constraints on organizational improvements," Journal of Management Studies, 19, 91-108, 1982.

Duncan, R. G. "Characteristics of organizational environments and perceived environmental uncertainty," Administrative Science Quarterly, 17 (2), 313-327 (a), 1972.

Elfring, T. and Volberda, H. W. "New Directions in Strategy: Beyond Fragmentation," London: Sage, 1998.

Hambrick, D. D. and Snow, Ch. C. "A contextual model of strategic decision making in organizations," Academy of Management Proceedings, 108-112, 1977.

Hatch, M. J. "The Dynamics of Organizational Culture," The Academy of Management Review 18 (4): 657-93, 1993.

Hatten, K. J. "Quantitative research methods in strategic management." In D. E. Schendel & C. W. Hofer (Eds.), Strategic management: A new view of business policy and planning. Boston: Little, Brown, 448-467, 1979.

Hart, S. L. "An Integrative Framework for Strategy-Making Process," Academy of Management Review, Vol 17/2, 327-351, 1992.

Hofer, C. W. "Some preliminary research on patterns of strategic behavior," Academy of Management Proceedings, 46-59, 1973.

Kuhn, T. S. The Structure of Scientific Revolutions. Chicago: University of Chicago Press, 1970.

Lawrence, P. and Lorsch, J. "Organization and environment." Boston: Division of Research, Harvard Business School, 1967.

Lindblom, C. E. "The Science of 'Muddling Through.'" Public Administration Review, 19: 78-88, 1959.

Masson, R. O. and I. Mitroff. Challenging Strategic Planning Assumptions. New York: John Wiley, 1981.

Maturana, H. and F. Varela. Autopoiesis and Cognition: The Realization of the Living. London: Reidl, 1980.

Meyerson M. and Banfield E. "Politics, planning and the public interest.," Glencoe, IL: Free Press, 1955.

Miller, D. "Evolution and Revolution: A Quantum View of Structural Change in Organizations." Journal of Management Studies, 19, 131-151, 1982.

Miller, D. "Configurations of Strategy and Structure: Towards a Synthesis." Strategic Management Journal, 7, 233-249, 1986.

Miller, D., "Configurations revisted." Strategic Management Journal, Chichester, Vol. 17, Iss. 7, pg. 505, 8 pgs., Jul 1996.

Miller, D. and Friesen, P. H. "Strategy-Making and Environment: The Third Link." Strategic Management Journal, 4, b:221-235, 1982.

Mintzberg, H. "The Strategy Concept 1: Five Ps for Strategy." California Management Review, 30, 1: 11-24, June 1987.

Mintzberg, H., Ashland, B. and Lampel, J. "Strategy Safari: A guided tour through the Wilds of Strategic Management." The Free Press, 1998.

Mitroff, I. I., Emshoff, J. R. "On strategic assumption-making: A dialectical approach to policy and planning." Academy of Management Review, 4, 1-13, 1979.

Morgan, G. "Paradigms, Metaphors and Puzzle Solving in Organization Theory." Administrative Science Quarterly, 25: 605-622, 1980.

Oswald S. L., Mossholfer K. W., Harris, S. G., "Relations between Strategic Involvement and Managers' perceptions of environment and competitive strengths." Group & Organization Management; Thousand Oaks, Sep 1997.

Pfeffer, J., and Salancik, G. R. *The External Control of Organizations: A Resource Dependence Perspective*, New York: Harper & Row, 1978.

Pfeffer, J. Management as symbolic action: The creation and maintenance of organizational paradigms. In L. L. Cummings & B. M. Staw (Eds.). *Research in organizational behavior*. Greenwood, C.T: JAI Press, 1-52, 1981.

Porter, M. E. Competitive Strategy: Techniques for Analyzing Industries and Competitors, New York, Free Press, 1980.

Prahalad, C. K. and Bettis, R. A. "The Dominant Logic: A New Linkage Between Diversity and Performance." Strategic Management Journal, 7: 485-501, 1986.

Prahalad, C. K. and Hamel, G. "The core Competence of the Corporation." Harvard Business Review, 68, 3: 79-91, June 1990.

Quinn, J. B. "Strategic Change: Logical incrementalism." Sloan Management Review, 20 (1): 7-21, 1978.

Quinn, J. B. *Strategies for Change: Logical Incrementalism*, Homewood, IL: Irwin, 1980a.

Rumelt, R. P. " The Evaluation of Business Strategy." In H. Mintzberg and J. B. Quinn, *The Strategy Process*, 3d ed., Englewood Cliffs, NJ: Prentice Hall, 1997.

Schon, D. A. *Invention and the Evolution of Ideas*. London: Tavistock, 1963.

Schon, D. A. "Generative Metaphor: A Perspective on Problem Setting in Sobrisge: Cambridge University Press, 1979.

Selznick, P. *Leadership in Administration: A Sociological Interpretation*, Evanston, IL: Row, Peterson, 1957.

Shrivatava, P. and Mitroff, I., "Enhancing Organizational Research Utilization: The Role of Decision Maker's Assumptions." Academy of Management Review, Vol. 9/1, 18-26,1984.

Smircich, L. and Morgan G. "Leadership: The management of meaning." Journal of Allied Behavior Science, 18 (3), 257-273, 1982.

Smircich, L. and Stubbart, C. "Strategic Management in an Enacted World." Academy of Management Review, 10, 4: 724-736, 1985.

Starbuck, W. H. "Congealing oil: Inventing ideologies to justify acting ideologies out." Journal of Management Studies, 19, 3-27, 1982.

Thomas, K. and Tymon, A. "The necessary qualities of relevant research: Lessons from recent criticisms of organizational science." Academy of Management Review, 7, 345-352, 1982.

Thompson, J. D. "Organizations in action." New York: Mc Graw-Hill, 1967.

Thorelli, H. B., *The Ecology of Organizations, Integral Strategy*, JAI Press, 1995.

Weick, K. E. "The social psychology of organizing." Reading. Mass: Addison-Wesley, 1969.

Weick, K. E. *The Social Psychology of Organizing*, Reading, MA: Addison-Wesley, first edition 1969, second edition 1979.

Weick, K. E. and Draft, R. L. The effectiveness of interpretation systems. In K. S. Cameron & D. A. Whetten (Eds.), *Organizational effectiveness: A comparison of multiple models.* New York: Academic Press, 71-93, 1983.

Wernerfelt, B. "A Resource-based View of the Firm." Strategic Management Journal, 5: 171-180, 1984.

Weiss, C. H. and Bucuvalas, M. J. "Truth tests and utility tests: Decision-makers frames of reference for social science research." American Sociological Review, 45, 302-314, 1980.

An Exploratory Analysis
of CRM Implementation Models

Stephan C. Henneberg

University of Bath, United Kingdom

SUMMARY. Customer Relationship Management (CRM) as a concept is a well-researched area of marketing theory. Since the 1990s the use of relational marketing approaches in consumer markets has found many managerial applications. However, the implementation considerations of CRM remained under-researched from a conceptual perspective, especially as implementation of many CRM projects are perceived as providing limited success. By using an exploratory, qualitative, research design, principally based on a Delphi methodology, this study highlights some crucial aspects of CRM implementation. Two clear CRM implementation foci can be distinguished: a dominant "hard" implementation of CRM (focussing on analytics, centralisation, and campaign management) and a "soft" implementation of CRM (focussing on decentralised customer experience management at the touch point level). Further analysis of the "hard" implementation model shows that companies using this path often have only a vague strategic understanding of the CRM

Stephan C. Henneberg, PhD, is Lecturer in Marketing, School of Management, University of Bath. His research and publication foci are in strategic management, marketing theory, CRM, and political marketing. He has extensive applied experience in the field of strategic marketing and customer relationship management through his work as a consultant with A.T. Kearney and McKinsey & Co.

Address correspondence to: S. C. M. Henneberg, School of Management, University of Bath, BA2 7AY United Kingdom (E-mail: s.c.m.henneberg@bath.ac.uk).

[Haworth co-indexing entry note]: "An Exploratory Analysis of CRM Implementation Models." Henneberg, Stephan C. Co-published simultaneously in *Journal of Relationship Marketing* (Best Business Books, an imprint of The Haworth Press, Inc.) Vol. 4, No. 3/4, 2005, pp. 85-104; and: *The Future of Relationship Marketing* (ed: David Bejou, and Adrian Palmer) Best Business Books, an imprint of The Haworth Press, Inc., 2005, pp. 85-104. Single or multiple copies of this article are available for a fee from The Haworth Document Delivery Service [1-800-HAWORTH, 9:00 a.m. - 5:00 p.m. (EST). E-mail address: docdelivery@haworthpress.com].

http://www.haworthpress.com/web/JRM
doi:10.1300/J366v04n03_06

project in place before they define the process and technical requirements. An implication of this finding is that standard IT processes are often used to derive strategic CRM guidelines, a reversal of a prescriptive "best-practice" implementation process. The implications and limitations of the findings as well as the need for further research is discussed. *[Article copies available for a fee from The Haworth Document Delivery Service: 1-800-HAWORTH. E-mail address: <docdelivery@haworthpress.com> Website: <http://www.HaworthPress.com> © 2005 by The Haworth Press, Inc. All rights reserved.]*

KEYWORDS. Customer relationship management, Delphi-Method, CRM implementation, process management

INTRODUCTION

Recently, relational marketing has become a focus of marketing theory (Bruhn 2003). Although extensively discussed in the academic literature since the beginning of the 1970s, the interest in relationship management for products and services in a mass marketing environment is a recent event (Battacharya and Bolton, 2000; Pels, 1999; Sheth and Parvatiyar, 1995; Sheth and Parvatiyar, 2000a; for a critique of these developments O'Malley and Tynan, 1999). It is grounded in work on business-to-business marketing relationships by the International Marketing and Purchasing Group (IMP) (Hakansson and Snehota, 2000) and the Nordic School of Marketing's studies on services marketing (Grönroos, 2000). Utilising the developing "network-paradigm", this new emphasis on longer-term exchange relationships, based on commitment and trust, caught the interest of traditional consumer marketers and practitioners during the mid-1990s. Faced with higher acquisition costs and satiated markets, leading to an increased importance of customer loyalty (Lemon et al., 2002; Reichheld, 1996a; Reichheld, 1996b; Winer, 2001), marketing practice and also marketing theory made customer relationship marketing (CRM) a focus of their efforts. This was further facilitated by new IT capabilities, e.g., in the area of database marketing and data-mining (Plakoyiannaki and Tzokas, 2002). While it has sometimes been argued that relationship marketing could transform marketing theory "beyond the 4Ps" by providing a new paradigm (Grönroos, 1994; Grönroos, 1997; Sheth, 2000), this has not happened (yet). However, many companies have enthusiastically taken to the concept as a way of becoming more customer-oriented (Bruhn, 2003;

Piercy, 2002). Investments in CRM projects have increased yearly; the annual spend on CRM (2001 data) is approximately $3.5-6 billion software costs and $20-34 billion system costs (Corner and Hinten, 2002; Ebner et al., 2002). Of significance, Forrester (2001) estimates higher, with a typical Global 3500 firm spending approximately $15-30 million per year on CRM activities. However, while theoretical studies of CRM (e.g., Bagozzi, 1995; Grönroos, 2000; Parvatiyar and Sheth, 2000; Peterson, 1995; Pels, 1999;) in addition to empirical studies relating to the concept of CRM are plentiful (DeWulf et al., 2001; Garbarino and Johnson, 1999), academic research on issues of implementation and on operational processes has largely been marginalised (Plakoyiannaki and Tzokas, 2002). For example, none of the 23 articles in the "Handbook of Relationship Marketing" (Sheth and Parvatiyar, 2000b) focus specifically on implementation issues. In addition, the managerial literature covers mostly IT-related issues of implementation (Leverick et al., 1998; Ling and Yen, 2001; Winer, 2001) and do not contribute to a holistic or conceptual analysis. Therefore, this paper focuses on two fundamental issues of CRM implementations: specifically, how are CRM projects implemented, along with, how can the often perceived shortcomings of many CRM implementations be explained. To tackle the first issue, the most commonly used CRM implementation path is identified. A discussion of the second issue is informed by an analysis of the underlying processes for this implementation path. This is done by comparing the actual measures taken against a normative CRM implementation model derived from a consensus of relevant managers.

CRM–
PANACEA OR PANDORA'S BOX OF MARKETING?

CRM and relational marketing activities, in general, have enthusiastically been adopted by organisations. Furthermore, the academic literature describes it as a fundamentally new paradigm of marketing theory based on an interaction and network approach (Bagozzi, 1995; Chien and Moutinho, 2000; Grönroos, 1994; Grönroos, 1997; Gummesson, 1997). CRM is seen as providing many important elements of customer-orientation and market-orientation (Meldrum, 2000). CRM has been described as lying on one end of the marketing strategy continuum (Bruhn, 2003; Grönroos, 1997), with transactional marketing its counterpart. This "broad view" of relationship marketing (Parvatiyar and Sheth, 2000) encompasses marketing activities that are based on initiating and enhancing interactions between parties to achieve mutual exchange and the fulfillment of promises through cooperative/collaborative behaviour, in order to establish longer-term relationships at a value to all involved (Grönroos, 1997; Parvatiyar and Sheth, 2000; Ravald and Grönroos, 1996; Sheth and Parvatiyar, 1995).

CRM is often identified by focusing on the outcomes of customer relationship management, i.e., a long-term commitment and trust-based relationship that survives incidences of dissatisfaction on both sides (Morgan and Hunt, 1994). CRM provides companies with competencies that allow them to build sustainable positions of competitive advantage by using customer information sensibly, "locking-in" high value customers and to some extent insulating themselves from market forces and competition (Oliver, 1999). These performance enhancements and their resulting positive effect on the company's profit margin also induce the development of systemic virtuous circles, e.g., via increased employee satisfaction, higher motivation, less staff turnover, and customer recommendations.

However, while there is enthusiasm about the concept of CRM, many managers perceive the CRM practice as unsatisfactory, too expensive, not delivering the desired results and in general disintegrating into large scale business process redesign and systems development efforts, i.e., a repetition of Enterprise Resource Planning (ERP) implementation shortcomings (Ebner et al., 2002). While the capital investments in CRM systems and processes are comparatively high, nearly all studies on the success of CRM have concluded that the perceived benefits and outcome are either ambiguous or negative. These studies show, for example, that only 20 percent of US financial institutions that have introduced CRM increased their profitability as a result (Ebner et al., 2002; Rigby et al., 2002). This view of CRM as a, generally, unsuccessful strategy is shared by many consumers (Fournier et al., 1998). Such results have caused some commentators to conclude that "[c]*ustomer relationship management is a failure*" (Mitchell, 2002, p. 30). However, most studies focus on managers' assessments of success while analytical constructs of measuring CRM effectiveness is still rare (see for an example Jain et al., 2002). In addition to the issue of unsatisfactory results, most CRM projects also cause major disruptions to the ongoing business of companies by drawing people and budget resources away from line-management responsibilities. New processes have to be learned, new routines developed which can cause efficiency and effectiveness decreases in the short-term (Ling and Yen, 2001). Therefore, CRM implementation is often described in the managerial literature as having many pitfalls (Hansotia, 2002; Ling and Yen, 2001). There is no clear understanding of different implementation paths for CRM, however, certain implementation elements, often described as CRM capabilities or competencies, are discussed. Ling and Yen (2001) identify three cornerstones of CRM: the knowledge or customer information platform; the customer interaction platform; and the tracking and feedback loops. For the purpose of the discussions as well as the analyses, this study was informed by the context of several distinct CRM capabilities as outlined in Plakoyiannaki and Tzokas (2002). They highlight five conceptual capabilities, derived from an axiomatic CRM process, which determine the success of a CRM system: learning/market orientation capabilities; integration capabilities; analytical capabilities; operational capabilities; and direction capabilities. These capabilities were used as an initial "*guiding tool*" (Plakoyiannaki and Tzokas, 2002, p. 234) and represent what Day (1994) describes as crucial "sensing" and "linking" capabilities for market-driven companies.

With all this in mind, it could be asked whether a major CRM implementation project resembles the opening of Pandora's box. In order to guide the research, two main exploratory research questions are proposed which are grounded in the literature review and the considerations on CRM which have been previously discussed:

RQ$_1$: How is a CRM implementation project usually approached by companies; where are the implementation foci?

RQ$_2$: Does the CRM implementation follow a "best-practice implementation approach" or can the perceived shortcomings in the outcomes potentially be explained by a deviation from this process?

While the first proposition is more concerned with a conceptual issue, which is of academic interest, the latter is meant to directly inform practitioner applications of CRM implementations.

RESEARCH METHODOLOGY

To answer the outlined exploratory research questions a qualitative research design was chosen, based on a judgmental consensus methodology. To collect data, in-depth interviews and Delphi studies were conducted. This research procedure is comparable with studies on implementation issues (Corner and Hinton, 2002; Larreche and Montgomery, 1977; Kincade et al., 2001) and its qualitative nature allows for a flexible framework to indicate root-causes as well as the integration of knowledge from "experts" for specific issues (Saunders et al., 2000). This methodology was specifically chosen as it is considered appropriate in innovative cross-case situations, although it has hitherto not received attention in marketing studies (Huberman and Miles, 1994; Story et al., 2001). Furthermore, the qualitative and exploratory nature of this study will inform further detailed studies on CRM implementation. Quantitative research results, a by-product of this study for illustrative purposes, are shown briefly below where appropriate.

Twenty-three companies, in three countries (Germany, UK, and France), took part in this study. Each of these companies was chosen because it had already finished at least the first stage of a major CRM implementation project in the last 5 years (around three-quarters of all companies finished their CRM implementation not longer than 25 months ago). The companies cover across most major industry sectors and have turnovers of between around EUR 100 million and EUR 80 billion (median approximately EUR 4 billion).

The participating managers, of between three and six per company, were all involved in their organisation's original CRM project. However, they were chosen to represent different managerial levels (e.g., Chief Information Officer, Chief Marketing Officer, but also customer segment managers and IT analysts) as well as functional departments (e.g., marketing, customer service, IT). For an overview of the research process see Figure 1. An initial phase (phase 1) involved two-hour face-to-face semi-structured interviews with the participating managers in all twenty-three companies, plus, in most cases, one-hour telephone follow-up interviews. An analysis of provided material regarding the CRM implementation study (e.g., strategy papers; CRM business requirement documents; requests for proposals) supplemented these interviews. This initial phase can be seen as in line with the recommended unstructured preparatory step for a classical Delphi study, the so-called "*experience survey*" (Story et al., 2001, p. 495). The data management of the interview transcripts was informed by a "loose" and inductive approach (Huberman and Miles, 1994), aided by the use of qualitative research software (in this case NUDIST). The second phase focussed on sixteen companies that had followed a certain implementation methodology ("hard" implementation). Between three and six managers (from different functions and hierarchy levels) were used for a Delphi-study. Four individual iterative rounds (i.e., three synthesis rounds) proved to be satisfactory to gain agreement between all participating managers

FIGURE 1. Research Process Outline

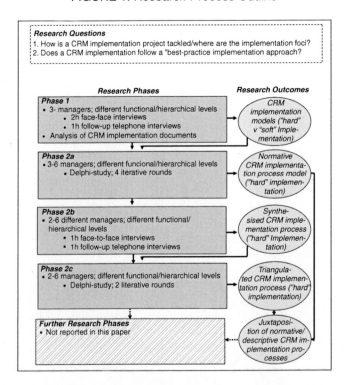

(phase 2a). The outcome of this Delphi-study, a normative CRM implementation process model, was then juxtaposed with data regarding the
implementation process of the CRM project in the individual companies. For this purpose, between two and six further interviews with key
managers (again from different functions and hierarchy levels) were
conducted (phase 2b). A synthesised process model was returned to
these managers for triangulation to initiate another Delphi-round (two
iterations) to assess whether or not this model represents their experiences with the CRM project (phase 2c). The used Delphi methodology
can be classified as a Classical Delphi study (Story et al., 2001).

All phases were conducted between Aug. 2002 and Jan. 2003 and the
Delphi studies were administered principally via e-mail. Such an e-mail/
online survey methodology is consistent with the context of this investigation and provides a quick, reliable and low cost method for delivery
(Sheehan and McMillan, 1999; Shough and Yates, 2002; Tse 1998).

The initial e-mail was embedded within a cover letter by the respective CEO or superior line manager. This contributed to an initial response rate of 63%. Respondents sent back the Delphi survey by return-email, if need be prompted by up to two reminder e-mails/telephone calls (Schaefer and Dillman, 1998). The "mortality" of respondents during the different Delphi rounds and research phases was below three percent. These high response rates and low mortality rates are in line with reports by some researchers that respondents view online surveys to be more important compared to traditional (mailed) surveys, increasing the likelihood that respondents respond to this survey method (Szymanski and Hise, 2000). It is equally important to recognise that there are some limitations of email surveys and these may have important consequences in the interpretation of survey findings. Szymanski and Hise (2000) assert that online surveys should not be long; consequently, constructs under investigation must be captured parsimoniously.

Although the participating managers contributed heavily to the research outcome, the researcher supervised, analysed, and synthesised specific decision points in the research process following the research methodology and prescribed outcome syntheses and interpretations. These decision points were the analysis of the dominant CRM implementation paths, and the analysis of the de-facto CRM implementation process (see Figure 1).

RESEARCH RESULTS

Phase 1. CRM Implementation Paths

In phase 1 the research project investigated a range of CRM projects and their implementation paths from a macro-perspective, i.e., used a strategic view. At this level the interviews indicated clearly that two "wide" constructs seem to characterise most CRM implementation projects. These constructs can be described as the development of "analytical CRM capabilities" ("hard" implementation) on the one hand and "customer experience management" ("soft" implementation) on the other. Under the analytical dimension managers usually subsume elements of an integrated customer database with marketing data-marts, a shared data model, marketing analysis and data-mining tools (e.g., propensity models for targeting and triggering activities), centralised CRM and campaign management functions, the integration of all touch-points/channels with feedback-loops to the centralised database, a standardisation of customer interaction and service processes via treatment strategies. The main implementation activities are software adaptation and integration, process redefinition, organisational integration, and analytical campaign management capabilities. It is often claimed that it "is significantly easier to gear up for CRM if marketing is a centralised activity and owns the customer relationship" (Hansotia, 2002, p. 123). This is counter to the conceptual core of CRM as a cross-functional orientation (Ryals, 2000), and constitutes one of the theoretical problems with this implementation construct.

The customer experience dimension encompasses aspects of direct customer interaction management. It is less "headquarter-oriented" and more decentralised. New customer interaction skills and strategies, a deep understanding of customer or customer segment relationship needs, the development of new customer-centric touch-points, and the ability to use the customer information to foster relationships are the focus of this implementation strategy. It is characterised by less detailed planning and loose frameworks (directional strategies) that are filled in on touch-point level. The main implementation activities are skill advancement, process and positioning development definition, exchange of lessons learned in test pilots, and the development of ways of how to capture customer information as part of the interaction routine.

It is noteworthy that the "hard" and "soft" CRM implementation constructs overlap to some extent with the experience described by Schultz (2000). He postulates an "American" CRM version (technology-based, analytics and SFA-driven and consequently focused on new customer acquisition) and juxtaposes it with a "Nordic" (i.e., Scandinavian and Northern European) CRM version (organisational structure-based and focused on retention and loyalty).

Referring these findings back to the initial capability context (Plakoyiannaki and Tzokas, 2002), Table 1 summarises the characteristics of the two implementation paths and illustrates their specific capability foci as derived from the interviews of phase 1. While there was mention of all five of the capability classes for most companies, the importance of certain competencies was clearly different by the specific CRM implementation path. Analytical and integration capabilities were the foci of a "hard" approach. Conversely, there was little emphasis on direction, i.e., a clear "top-down" process of strategic CRM aims being transformed into tactical activities and processes (e.g., campaigns, service levels, treatment strategies). For a "soft" implementation on the other hand, directional capabilities were one of the key implementation ele-

TABLE 1. Relative Implementation Importance of CRM Capabilities for Different CRM Implementation Paths

	"Hard" CRM Implementation	"Soft" CRM Implementation
1. *learning/market orientation capabilities*	important	very important
2. *integration capabilities*	very important	important
3. *analytical capabilities*	very important	somewhat important
4. *operational capabilities*	important	important
5. *direction capabilities*	somewhat important	very important

ments in order to provide a clear framework for the unstructured and de-centralised CRM activities. While analytical capabilities *per se* only play a secondary role for a "soft" CRM implementation, the cultural elements of a market-orientation and a learning environment play a major part in the implementation activities.

However, most managers (74 percent) agreed that a payback (i.e., an amortisation of CRM investments) was only possible if a CRM system delivered certain aspects of both dimensions. However, 68 percent of all managers also stated that because of implementation issues of complexity, resource availability, etc., a focus on one of the two dimensions in the first phase(s) of a CRM implementation was necessary. Within the sample of CRM implementation projects, most companies had focused their implementation efforts on "hard" CRM implementation issues. Of the twenty-three companies, 16 (70 percent) were clearly using a "hard" implementation model, while four (17 percent) were clearly "soft". Three companies could not be clearly classified within these two categories and were therefore labelled a "hybrid" approach towards CRM implementation. No significant differences by industry sector could be identified. However, this could be due to the low number of cases. The "hard" implementation strategy supports the characteristics that are most often identified in the managerial literature on CRM implementation: data-warehouse-driven, centralised, integrated (Hansotia, 2002; Ling and Yen, 2001; Rigby et al., 2002; Winer, 2001).

Most managers in the sample were not satisfied with the outcome of the CRM implementation. They classified the results of their CRM projects in the majority as either "dissatisfied" (45 percent) or "very dissatisfied" (7 percent). On the other hand, only 6% were very satisfied, 17% satisfied, and 25% indifferent. A cross-tabulation with the chosen implementation path shows that there is no significant association between implementation success and implementation path (predictive association $\lambda = 0.19$ for the implementation path as dependent variable). Nevertheless, as indicated by the much smaller number of "totally dissatisfied" managers for "soft" implementations, a tentative proposition can be constructed, stating that "soft" CRM projects have less implementation risk under certain circumstances. Further research with larger samples would be needed to corroborate this proposition.

Phase 2: CRM Implementation Process

In the phases that followed, the focus was on companies that choose to use a "hard" implementation path. This decision was made as the "hard" implementation path was the norm and there were not enough companies in the sample that used a "soft" implementation. A microview on the process level was used, due to the fact that the macro-view of different CRM implementation paths did not explain the general dissatisfaction with these implementation projects. A more detailed analysis of the implementation process itself is therefore deemed necessary to understand some of the issues that contribute to the high perceived failure rate of the analysed CRM implementations. A focus on implementation processes in contrast to structure and administration is suggested in the literature (Cespedes and Piercy, 1996) that corresponds with the opinions of the managers.

To establish a normative process benchmark, the Delphi-study of phase 2a resulted in the process model for a "hard" CRM implementation (see Figure 2). As anticipated, this normative process showed considerable overlap with suggested best-practice CRM implementation processes (Ling and Yen, 2001).

To compare this normative process with a representation of how the CRM implementation had been conducted, a different set of managers developed a descriptive process model of the CRM implementation, as they perceived it had happened in their companies'. Via a triangulation round this descriptive model reached an abstract level that captured the essence, if not the details, of the implementation process of the sixteen companies that used a "hard" implementation. The descriptive CRM implementation process can be found in Figure 3.

FIGURE 2. Normative CRM Implementation Process Model for "Hard" Implementation (Outcome of Phase 2a)

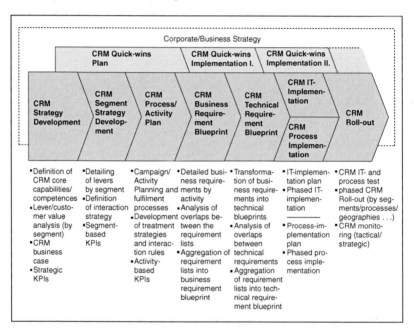

What is apparent when one compares the two processes is that the descriptive process model shows characteristics of being truncated at the front, when compared with the prescriptive model. The linear process model of the prescriptive model contrasts with the more chaotic and counter-intuitive referentiality of the descriptive model. The following elements can be characterised as having a crucial difference: While the prescriptive model is anchored in a clear strategic framework down to detailed segment plans from which process and activity plans are derived, i.e., a clear understanding about what the company wants to achieve through CRM, these phases are not significant in the descriptive model. Most managers acknowledge that strategic considerations were neglected (82%), that the consensus of what the company wanted to do with their CRM capability was superficial at the start of the implementation process (66%). This is illustrated by identifying that only 20 percent of the companies had prioritised CRM levers and target segments, only 12 percent had segment-based CRM activity plans while only 20 percent had any strate-

FIGURE 3. Descriptive CRM Implementation Process Model (Outcome of Phase 2c)

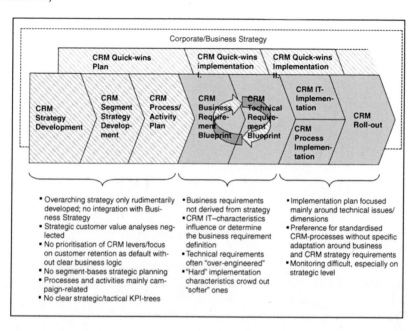

gic CRM key performance indicators (KPIs). The consequence of these shortcomings was important in the subsequent process phases. Where the prescriptive model continues with the development of business and technical requirement blueprints which are "conditioned" by the detailed strategic considerations, the descriptive models *de facto* starts the detailed implementation process by defining the business requirements. However, as the strategic standards set are only "high-level" and therefore rather opaque, the guidance for the development of these blueprints are often influenced or even determined by the characteristics of standard CRM software packages. In effect, this is the business equivalent to the so-called naturalistic fallacy of "This is the way it is, therefore, this is also the way it should be". One Chief Marketing Officer recalls that his company wrote their CRM business requirement blueprint in retrospect after they had analysed an IT vendor proposal. A possible effect of this might be that 60 percent of the managers believe that their CRM solution is not specific to their company requirements and 73 percent believe it is "over-engineered". Referring to CRM IT-package descriptions and vendor proposals also obviates many CRM characteristics of a "soft" implementation. Consequently, the implementation is focused very much around software as well as technical integration issues that subsequently may have further implications on organisational structure and skill issues. Due to the limited strategic planning, the rollout phase in the descriptive model shows signs of being controlled only on a tactical level without strategic monitoring. It was identified that 46 percent of managers stated that there was no evaluation of strategic milestones within the first 6-8 months of rollout. An additional element of the descriptive versus the prescriptive model lies in the absence of implementation-accompanying quick-win programmes that might test CRM content or processes, build skills and create acceptance of CRM within the company.

The truncatedness of the strategy process is something that the implementation literature normally does not anticipate; the strategy is seen as a distinct phase which maybe misunderstood, but usually not neglected (Cespedes and Piercy, 1996) or retrospectively filled-in. However, a recent McKinsey study agrees that "[a] failure to establish clear business goals before launching a CRM effort is the most common and important source of these problems" (Ebner et al., 2002, p. 51). This is mirrored by other management consultancies, e.g., Bain (Rigby et al., 2002) as well as by analyses of the main factors linked to implementation effectiveness of IT marketing projects (Leverick et al., 1998).

It is noteworthy that traditional issues related to marketing implementation failure did not feature prominently in the managerial opinions. The "fit" discussion of organisational structure and strategic choice, as well as budgeting and resource issues and control systems which are conventionally discussed in the literature (Bourgeois and Brodwin, 1984; Cespedes and Piercy, 1996), did not inform this analysis in any substantial way.

What becomes apparent from the above analysis is that there are clear signs that the "hard" CRM implementation processes are falling short of the desired prescription. This can be seen as possibly a determining, or at least a contributing, factor to the dissatisfaction with the outcome of CRM projects. The truncated implementation process might be a direct outflow of a thinking anchored in beliefs such as: "The major focus of CRM is on the technology platform . . . " (Hansotia, 2002, p. 125).

CONCLUSION

Summary and Managerial Implications

In this study some aspects of the implementation of CRM projects were analysed using an exploratory and qualitative methodology based mainly on the Delphi-method. Informed by two main research questions, the results can be summarised as follows. Most companies in the sample choose to approach CRM implementation projects by focusing on analytical competencies, an integrated IT platform and centralised organisational structure, characterised as a "hard" implementation approach. A "soft" approach, based on customer experience management, utilising a decentralised, interaction and learning skills-based approach, was rare, although successful CRM is deemed by managers to consist of elements of both dimensions. These two implementation paths seem to be the main foci of CRM implementation projects. In scrutinising the "hard" CRM implementation approach further, a comparison between a consensual "best-practice approach" and the actual implementation phases showed clearly that the strategy definition phase plus some strategy-connected phases were implemented only to a very limited depth and level of detailing in most analysed CRM projects. CRM IT-processes appear to have played a crucial aspect in framing the business requirement definitions in many "hard" implementation projects, resulting in a lack of overall guidance and monitoring activities. This truncated implementation process can be hypothesised as a contributing factor to the perceived inadequance of many CRM implementations. Referring to Plakoyiannaki and Tzokas (2002) analogy of CRM implementations with an "*odyssey*" (p. 235), one must conclude that most companies do not seem to have a clear understanding of their "CRM trip" in advance. These findings have certain direct managerial implications. The CRM implementation needs to be "front-loaded" in order to achieve maximal guidance of the following implementation process as well as allowing for a comprehensive monitoring process during and after the implementation. As part of the CRM strategy development, a clear understanding of the implementation focus, i.e., "hard" versus "soft," needs to be agreed upon to allow a streamlined and guided process.

Limitations and Contributions of This Study

The main contributions of this study are twofold: first, it analyses and categorises the often under-researched area of CRM implementations by highlighting two dominant implementation paths. Second, it juxtaposes management practice in CRM implementations with "best-practice" standards, highlighting the truncated nature of the former in comparison with the latter. In particular, the findings are a qualification of the literature on the strategy formulation-implementation dichotomy (Cespedes, 1991) that sees strategy and implementation as part of one process but in two distinct stages (Cespedes and Piercy, 1996). This research identifies the intricate nature of the interplay between implementation and strategy formulation *in realiter*, e.g., the fact that in "hard" implementation projects the standardised CRM software processes might influence or even determine the business requirement formulation.

However, it is important to highlight the limitations of this study in order to put further research propositions into perspective. The mainly qualitative and exploratory nature of this study brings with it a limited generalisability of the conclusions. The findings should be used as pointers for further research. As the data for case studies of the "soft" implementation model were very limited, no further analyses regarding the implementation process could be gained from them and all subsequent conclusions are specific to the "hard" CRM implementation model. Furthermore, the findings that CRM is often implemented in a "truncated" way in comparison to normative implementation approaches should not cause managers to overemphasise the impact of rigid planning. As the strategy literature informs us, an informal and learning-based approach (Argyris, 1989) to strategy implementation, using adaptive and directional guidance frameworks only (Beinhocker, 1999) might be a better way than a cartesianistic and rational planning model, (for an overview of the strategy theory/implementation landscape see Mintzberg and Lampel, 1999). Such an "emerging" strategy implementation process nevertheless emphasises strategic considerations as pivotal in the focusing of implementation activities (Eisenhardt, 1999).

Research Propositions

Because of the exploratory character of this study, many further research propositions can be derived from the discussions above. The most intriguing question was offered by the participating managers themselves. When being given the results of the study, they proposed the following hypotheses that have been synthesised in the following implementation model (see Figure 4).

FIGURE 4. Hypothetical CRM Implementation Model

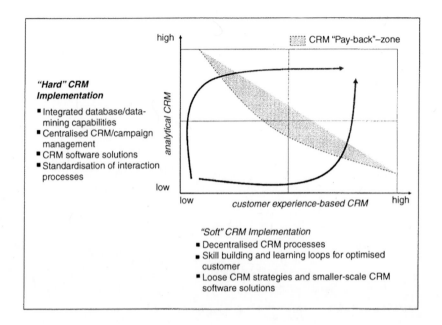

The core elements of this hypothetical CRM implementation model are:

- A CRM implementation needs to focus on one of the two generic implementation paths in order to be successful.
- Which implementation is more likely to be successful depends on the company situation (i.e., existing capabilities and skills, customer expectations)
- The initial focus on one of the two implementation foci is not enough to allow the company to make the CRM project successful, i.e., get into the "pay-back zone". Although there are examples for companies that use "uni-dimensional CRM" successfully, e.g., Capital One for a hard CRM focus and Nordstroem for a soft focus), companies need CRM follow-up projects that supplement the initially created CRM capabilities with complementary elements.

REFERENCES

Argyris, C. (1989). *Strategy Implementation: An Experience in Learning*, Organisational Dynamics, Vol. 18/2, pp. 5-15.

Bagozzi, R. P. (1995). *Reflections on Relationship Marketing in Consumer Markets*, Journal of the Academy of Marketing Science, Vol. 23/4, pp. 272-277.

Beinhocker, E. D. (1999). *Robust Adaptive Strategies*, Sloan Management Review, Spring, pp. 95-106.

Bhattacharya, C. B./Bolton, R. N. (2000). *Relationship Marketing in Mass Markets*, in J. N. Sheth, A. Parvatiyar (eds.), Handbook of Relationship Marketing, Sage, Thousand Oaks, pp. 327-354.

Bourgeois, L.; Brodwin, D. (1984). *Strategic Implementation: Five Approaches to an Elusive Phenomenon*, Strategic Management Journal, Vol. 5, pp. 241-264.

Bruhn, M. (2003). *Relationship Marketing*, Prentice Hall, Harlow.

Cespedes, F. V. (1991). *Organizing and Implementing the Marketing Effort*, Addison-Wesley, Reading.

Cespedes, F. V.; Piercy, N. F. (1996). *Implementing Marketing Strategy*, Journal of Marketing Management, Vol. 12, pp. 135-160.

Chien, C. S.; Moutinho, L. (2000). *The External Contingency and Internal Characteristic of Relationship Marketing*, Journal of Marketing Management, Vol. 16, 583-595.

Corner, I.; Hinton, M. (2002). *Customer Relationship Management System: Implementation Risks and Relationship Dynamics*, Qualitative Market Research, N. 4, Vol. 5, pp. 239-251.

Day, G. S. (1994). *The Capabilities of Market-Driven Organizations*, Journal of Marketing, Vol. 58, Oct. pp. 37-52.

DeWulf, K.; Odekerken-Schroeder, G.; Iacobucci, D. (2001). *Investment in Consumer Relationships: A Cross-Country and Cross-Industry Exploration*, Journal of Marketing, Vol. 65, Oct., pp. 33-50.

Ebner, M.; Hu, A.; Levitt, D.; McCrory, J. (2002). *How to Rescue CRM*, McKinsey Quarterly, Special Edition: Technology, pp. 49-57.

Eisenhardt, K. M. (1999). *Strategy as Strategic Decision Making*, Sloan Management Review, Spring, pp. 65-72.

Fontana, A.; Frey, J. H. (1994). *Interviewing*, in N. K. Denzin, Y. S. Lincoln (eds.), Handboock of Qualitative Research, Sage, Thousand Oaks, pp. 361-376.

Forrester (2001). *CRM: At What Cost?*, Forrester Report, March.

Fournier, S.; Dobscha, S.; Mick. D. G. (1998). *Preventing the Premature Death of Relationship Marketing*, Harvard Business Review, Jan-Feb, pp. 42-51.

Garbarino, E.; Johnson, M. S. (1999). *The Different Roles of Satisfaction, Trust, and Commitment in Customer Relationships*, Journal of Marketing, Vol. 63, April, pp. 70-87.

Grönroos, C. (1994). *Quo Vadis, Marketing? Towards a Relationship Marketing Paradigm*, Journal of Marketing Management, Vol. 10, pp. 347-360.

Grönroos, C. (1997). *From Marketing Mix to Relationship Marketing: Towards a Paradigm Shift in Marketing*, Management Decision, Vol. 35/4, pp. 322-339.

Grönroos, C. (2000). *Relationship Marketing: The Nordic School Perspective*, in J. N. Sheth, A. Parvatiyar (eds.), Handbook of Relationship Marketing, Sage, Thousand Oaks, pp. 95-118.

Gummesson, E. (1997). *Relationship Marketing as a Paradigm Shift: Some Conclusion from the 30R Approach*, Management Decision, Vol. 35/4, pp. 267-272.

Hakansson, H.; Snehota, I. J. (2000). *The IMP Perspective: Assets and Liabilities of Business Relationships*, in J. N. Sheth, A. Parvatiyar (eds.), Handbook of Relationship Marketing, Sage, Thousand Oaks, pp. 69-94.

Hansotia, B. (2002). *Gearing up for CRM: Antecedents to Successful Implementation*, Journal of Database Marketing, Vol. 10/2, pp. 121-132.

Huberman, A. M.; Miles, M. B. (1994). *Data Management and Analysis Methods*, in N. K. Denzin; Y. S. Lincoln (eds.), Handbook of Qualitative Research, Sage, Thousand Oaks, pp. 428-444.

Jain R.; Jain, S.; Dhar, U. (2002). *Measuring Customer Relationship Management*, Journal of Services Research, Vol. 2/2, pp. 97-109.

Larreche, J.-C.; Montgomery, D. B. (1977). *A Framework for the Comparison of Marketing Models: A Delphi Study*, Journal of Marketing Research, Vol. 14, pp. 487-498.

Lemon, K. N.; Whit, T. B.: Winer, R. S. (2002). *Dynamic Customer Relationship Management: Incorporating Future Considerations into the Service Retention Decision*, Journal of Marketing, Vol. 66, Jan., pp. 1-14.

Leverick, F.; Littler, D.; Bruce, M.; Wilson, D. (1998). *Using Information Technology Effectively: A Study of Marketing Installations*, Journal of Marketing Management, Vol. 14, pp. 927-962.

Ling, R.; Yen, D. C. (2001). *Customer Relationship Management: An Analysis Framework and Implementation Strategies*, Journal of Computer Information Systems, Vo. 41/3, pp. 82-98.

Mitchell, A. (2002). *Customer Fall by Wayside as CRM Focuses on Costs*, Marketing Week, Vol. 25/50, pp. 30-31.

Morgan, R. M.; Hunt, S. D. (1994). *The Commitment-Trust Theory of Relationship Marketing*, Journal of Marketing, Vol. 58, July, pp. 20-38.

Meldrum, M. (2000). *A Market Orientation*, in Cranfield School of Management, Marketing Management: A Relationship Marketing Perspective, Palgrave, Basingstoke, pp. 3-16.

Mintzberg, H.; Lampel, J. (1999). *Reflecting on the Strategy Process*, Sloan Management Review, Spring, pp. 21-30.

Oliver, R. L. (1999). *Whence Consumer Loyalty?* Journal of Marketing, Vol. 63, Special Issue, pp. 33-44.

O'Malley, L.; Tynan, C. (1999). *The Utility of the Relationship Metaphor in Consumer Markets: A Critical Evaluation*, Journal of Marketing Management, Vol. 15, pp. 587-602.

Parvatiyar, A.; Sheth, J. N. (2000). *The Domain and Conceptual Foundations of Relationship Marketing*, in J. N. Sheth, A. Parvatiyar (eds.), Handbook of Relationship Marketing, Sage, Thousand Oaks, pp. 3-38.

Pels, J. (1999). *Exchange Relationship in Consumer Markets?* European Journal of Marketing, Vol. 33/1-2, pp. 19-37.

Peterson, R. A. (1995). *Relationship Marketing and the Consumer*, Journal of the Academy of Marketing Science, Vol. 23/4, pp. 278-281.

Piercy, N. F. (2002). *Market-led Strategic Change*, Butterworth-Heinemann, Oxford.

Plakoyiannaki, E.; Tzokas, N. (2002). *Customer Relationship Management: A Capabilities Portfolio Perspective*, Journal of Database Marketing, Vol. 9/3, pp. 228-237.

Ravald, A.; Grönroos, C. (1996). *The Value Concept and Relationship Marketing*, European Journal of Marketing, Vol. 30/2, pp. 19-30.

Reichheld, F. F. (1996a). *The Loyalty Effect*, Harvard Business School Press, Boston.

Reichheld, F. F. (1996b). *Learning from Customer Defections*, Harvard Business Review, March/April, pp. 56-69.

Rigby, D. K.; Reichheld, F. F.; Schefter, P. (2002). *Avoid the Four Perils of CRM*, Harvard Business Review, Feb., pp. 101-109.

Ryals, L. (2000). *Organizing for Relationship Marketing*, in Cranfield School of Management (Eds.), Marketing Management: A Relationship Marketing Perspective, Palgrave, Basingstoke, pp. 249-263.

Saunders, M.; Lewis, P.; Thornhill, A. (2000). *Research Methods for Business Students*, Prentice Hall, Harlow.

Schaefer, D. R.; Dillman, D. A. (1998). *Development of a Standard E-Mail Methodology*, Public Opinion Quarterly, Vol. 62, pp. 378-397.

Schultz, D. E. (2000). *Learn to Differentiate CRM's Two Faces*, Marketing News, 20. No. 2000, p. 11.

Sheehan, K. B.; McMillan, S. J. (1999). *Response Variation in E-Mail Surveys: An Exploration*, Journal of Advertising Research, Vol. 39/4, pp. 45-54.

Sheth, J. N. (2000). *Relationship Marketing: Paradigm Shift or Shaft*, in J. N. Sheth, A. Parvatiyar (eds.), Handbook of Relationship Marketing, Sage, Thousand Oaks, pp. 609-620.

Sheth, J. N.; Parvatiyar, A. (1995). *Relationship Marketing in Consumer Markets: Antecedents and Consequences*, Journal of the Academy of Marketing Science, Vol. 23/4, pp. 255-271.

Sheth, J. N.; Parvatiyar, A. (2000a). *The Evolution of Relationship Marketing*, in J. N. Sheth, A. Parvatiyar (eds.), Handbook of Relationship Marketing, Sage, Thousand Oaks, pp. 119-148.

Sheth, J. N.; Parvatiyar, A. (2000b). *Handbook of Relationship Marketing*, Sage, Thousand Oaks.

Shough, S.; Yates, D. (2002). *The Advantages of an E-Mail Survey*, The Journal of Applied Business Research, Vol. 18/2.

Story, V.; Hurdley, L.; Smith, G.; Saker, J. (2001). *Methodological and Practical Implications of the Delphi Technique in Marketing Decision-Making: A Re-Assessment*, The Marketing Review, Vol. 1, pp. 487-504.

Szymanski, D. M.; Hise, R. T. (2000). *e-Satifaction: An Initial Examination*, Journal of Retailing, Vol. 76/3, pp. 309-322.

Tse, A. C. B. (1998). *Comparing the Response Rate, Response Speed, Response Quality of Two Methods of Two Methods of Sending Questionnaires: e-Mail Versus Mail*, Journal of the Market Research Society, Vol. 40/4, pp. 353-361.

Winer, R. S. (2001). *A Framework for Customer Relationship Management*, California Management Review, Vol. 43/4, pp. 89-105.

Developing Buyer-Seller Relationships Through Face-to-Face Negotiations

Tracy G. Harwood

DeMontfort University, United Kingdom

SUMMARY. This paper reviews the findings of research into information exchange in real-life negotiations in business-to-business (B2B) relationships. Despite the recognition by both practitioners and academics of face-to-face negotiation as a core competence essential to the longevity of business relationships, there has been little research into verbal negotiator behaviour in this context. Based on observation of 12 substantive negotiations, wherein the parties were engaged in strategic relationship development, the findings indicate distinct patterns of verbal behaviour at different stages of relational development. This has important implications for the development of theory as well as the behavioural stances adopted by individuals engaged in relational development through the process of face-to-face negotiation.

It is contended that enhanced understanding of this important aspect of B2B relationships leads to the development of more closely aligned strategic plans which may improve return on relational investment. Findings may, therefore, be used as an aid to decision-making in devel-

---

Tracy G. Harwood, PhD, BA(Hons), MCIM, ILTM, is Senior Lecturer in Marketing, Leicester Business School, De Montfort University, The Gateway, Leicester LE1 9BH, United Kingdom (E-mail: tghmar@dmu.ac.uk).

[Haworth co-indexing entry note]: "Developing Buyer-Seller Relationships Through Face-to-Face Negotiations." Harwood, Tracy G. Co-published simultaneously in *Journal of Relationship Marketing* (Best Business Books, an imprint of The Haworth Press, Inc.) Vol. 4, No. 3/4, 2005, pp. 105-122; and: *The Future of Relationship Marketing* (ed: David Bejou, and Adrian Palmer) Best Business Books, an imprint of The Haworth Press, Inc., 2005, pp. 105-122. Single or multiple copies of this article are available for a fee from The Haworth Document Delivery Service [1-800-HAWORTH, 9:00 a.m. - 5:00 p.m. (EST). E-mail address: docdelivery@haworthpress.com].

oping business relationships which could, ultimately, lead to more effectively targeted planning for interactions and, potentially, greater outcome success. *[Article copies available for a fee from The Haworth Document Delivery Service: 1-800-HAWORTH. E-mail address: <docdelivery@haworthpress.com> Website: <http://www.HaworthPress.com> © 2005 by The Haworth Press, Inc. All rights reserved.]*

KEYWORDS. B2B, negotiation, relationships, face-to-face, information exchange

INTRODUCTION

Within the context of relationship marketing (RM), face-to-face negotiation remains a competence required of individuals involved in the management of strategically important B2B relationships. Indeed, it is a core competence essential to the longevity of business relationships. This paper firstly reviews the literature applicable to the research context, gives an overview of the research and then discusses the exchange of information in the real-life negotiations of 12 dyads of buyers and sellers engaged in the process of developing and managing long-term relationships between their organisations.

The findings of the research reveal distinct patterns of verbal behaviour at stages of relational development. The findings have important implications for managing relationships through the face-to-face negotiation process in order to enhance outcome success. This includes the development of interpersonal skills training of managers and alignment of strategies which improve the return on relational investment.

LITERATURE REVIEW

Value of Face-to-Face Negotiation

Within the context of classic marketing relationships (Gummesson, 1994), there is now wide acceptance of a paradigm shift from transaction-based marketing to RM (for a summary see eg., Veloutsou, Saren and Tzokas, 2002). Although exchange remains the premise of marketing, Gronroos (1996, 1997, 2001) highlights that the modern approach focuses on the value created for customers. Value in relationships is added throughout and is emergent from the process of exchange and, indeed, is clearly perceived by the parties engaged in the relationship. Such value includes commitment, trust, customer orientation, empathy, experience, satisfaction and communication (Conway and Swift, 2000; Hogg, Nutall, Long and Davison, 1998). In particular, Boles, Brashear, Bellenger and Barksdale (2000) found that value is added through the frequency of communications and physical proximity between buyers and sellers, while Lapierre (2000) identifies flexibility and responsiveness as key components.

The premise of RM is that the buying and selling parties co-operate and become dependent upon one another (Dwyer, Shurr and Oh, 1987). Ultimately, this leads to significantly improved financial and market performance (Ballantyne, Christopher and Payne, 2000), such that relationships may be seen as 'strategic assets' by the parties (Johnson, 1999). Drivers for evolution include the recognition that not all customers are the same; a move towards retention of customers, rather than acquisition of new (Reichheld and Sasser, 1990; Payne and Frow, 1997); the just-in-time concept leading towards greater openness between buyers and sellers (Donaldson, 1996; Zineldin, 2000); and, trends in outsourcing (Matthyssens and van den Bulte, 1994). Simultaneously, selling behaviour has evolved from personal selling for short-term goals to a 'life-long process' (Rich, 2000), moving away from commodity type transactions to bespoke solutions which require different approaches to salesmanship. Traditional models of objection handling (Strong, 1925) have given way to investigation of needs eg., the SPIN strategy (Rackham, 1987) and counsellor/consultative selling models (DeCormier and Jobber, 1998; Carlisle and Parker, 1989).

Negotiation is seen to be part of the sales cycle (e.g., Robinson, Faris and Wind, 1967), and is defined as "a process that is entered into by parties who wish and are able to reach a mutually satisfactory solution on the division of issues of common interest but on which they currently conflict. The solution is reached through a process of bargaining. There is an exchange of detailed information on the issues at stake incorporating the parties beliefs and expectations. Through techniques of argument and persuasion, a mutually acceptable decision is sought" (Harwood, 2003, p. 39). The literature on negotiation highlights two distinct approaches to achieving agreement: those reached through collaborative means and those reached through competitive means (e.g., Lewicki, Saunders and Minton, 1997; Murray, 1986; Fisher and Ury, 1981). It is characterised by elements of trust, risk-taking, power, flexibility and fairness that are used strategically and tactically to influence the outcome. Success is enhanced by thorough preparation and planning, and well developed skills in the art and science of negotiation (Raiffa, 1985, 1997), producing agreements that result in solutions which are tenable over time (Huthwaite, 1998).

Dwyer et al. (1987) emphasise the importance of the inter-personal interaction process in RM approaches. They recognised that much work has been done in the area of transactional or 'tactical' negotiations between buyers and sellers, and call for more to be done in the area of 'contractual' or 'structural' negotiations–an area which remains relatively untouched even today (Shaw, 1999; Keillor, Parker and Pettijohn, 2000). Veloutsou et al. (2002) also highlight the need for greater understanding of the relational behaviour within marketing relationships. This is an important point when considering the comments made by Keillor et al. (2000) who state the quality of interaction is a controllable determinant in satisfying customers. This is supported by Rich and Smith (2000) who contend that employers should look to the ability of salespeople to adapt their 'social styles' to better match the expectations of the customer. It is generally accepted that a closer relational match between individuals results in longer-lasting relationships.

Communication is the process by which business relationships are formed (Dwyer et al., 1987, Grönroos et al., 2001) comprising the exchange of information (see, e.g., Wren and Simpson, 1996; Sharma and Patterson, 1999). This can lead to the development of the underlying glue for relationships–trust and commitment (e.g., Wilkinson and Young, 1994; Millman, 1994; Peters and Fletcher, 1995; Lewicki, Saunders and Minton, 1997; Wren and Simpson, 1997; Hutt, Stafford, Walker and Reingen, 2000).

It has been suggested (Davenport, 1994) that up to two-thirds of information and operational knowledge derives from informal face-to-face interactions (Dougherty, 1999). Baiman, Rajan and Kanodia (2002) state that considerably more information is exchanged between parties engaged in a networked relationship than those engaged in an arms-length relationship, although make the important point that information exchanged even in an ongoing and close relationship could be exploited or 'misappropriated'. Hendon, Henson and Herbig (1999) have suggested that a typical senior manager spends around twenty percent of the working day engaged in negotiations which increases to over fifty percent if the manager is undertaking international business, while de Burca (2001) found this accounted for over eighty percent of contact.

Purdy and Nye's (2000) analysis of different communications media (face-to-face, videoconferencing, telephone and computer-mediated communication) found the most effective means in terms of outcome efficiency, time taken and satisfaction of the parties, was face-to-face interaction. These authors also found that face-to-face interaction was more likely to result in collaboration between the parties. A contention also supported by Valley (1999).

Marketing Networks

The Industrial Marketing and Purchasing Group's 'interaction approach' focuses on understanding ongoing business relationships and the 'interaction' between 'active' buyers and sellers and inter-organisational networks of business relationships (e.g., Ford et al., 2000). As interaction between individuals and groups of individuals from within buying and selling organisations unfolds over time (exchanges of goods, services, money, formal information or 'social chit-chat'), so the relationship between individuals and groups evolves the relationship. Interactions, or episodes, influence subsequent episodes, which must be managed to ensure the relationship thrives. Clearly, organisations will have a number of relationships which may be interdependent, requiring different levels of resourcing, effort and commitment to sustain.

In turn, this suggests the 'portfolio' of relationships must be carefully managed to ensure the relationships most closely meeting the strategic requirements of the organisation are fostered, since not all relationships will have the same level of return for the investing parties. The approach is expanded to encompass the network of relationships between buyers and sellers across the organisation and through the supply chain (which may include service providers, distributors, development partners, etc., see e.g., Healy, Hastings, Brown and Gardiner, 2001). The expansion of relationships to networks has received much attention in the literature (refer e.g., Iacobucci, 1996). Relationships do not 'happen' in isolation from one another–they are linked to others by virtue of the nature of an organisation i.e., they exist in symbiosis or co-exist (Bengtsson and Kock, 1999) and, as such, are inherently relational in nature. For example, managers will be engaged in more than one business relationship and will compare relative success of techniques, attitudes and approaches across these relationships (Ford et al., 2000). Indeed, this is a concept that has also been discussed in the context of negotiation (Ertel, 1999). Drivers for network analysis are the potentials for efficiencies and innovation, such as that found by Epinette, Petit and Vialla (1999) in their analysis of the global telecomms industry. This intimates a wider spectrum of relationships that span industries. Nonetheless, as Stern (1996) and Holt and McDonald (2001) state, the dyadic relationship, i.e., a relationship between two actors, remains the fundamental unit of analysis.

Relational Development

A structured approach to the analysis and management of dyadic relationships is found in the body of literature on relational development and key account management (KAM). It highlights the cyclic evolution of relationships from early stages of encounter or 'courtship' to partnership or 'marriage' and, ultimately, dissolution or 'divorce' (Ford, 1980; Wilson and Mummalaneri, 1986; Dwyer et al., 1987; Millman and Wilson, 1994, Grossman, 1998). Millman and Wilson's (1994) relational development model, which has subsequently been further researched (McDonald, Millman and Rogers, 1996; Wilson, 1999) and adapted (McDonald, 1998; Cheverton, 1999; McDonald, Rogers and Woodburn, 2000), proposes that relationships become increasingly collaborative between buyers and sellers as the complexity of the transactions increase, as intimated by Broderick (1998). The Millman-Wilson model, adapted from the earlier work of Ford (1980) and Dwyer et al (1987), proposes five stages of relational development in the context of strategically important business relationships, i.e., key account management (KAM), and one further stage of dissolution (uncoupling-KAM). The relational development stages are: Preparing for/pre-KAM; Early-KAM; Mid-KAM; Partnership-KAM and Synergistic-KAM.

The process of relational development revolves around trust and co-operation (Lamming, 1993). This is an aspect of relationship development that is inherently complex to implement because, as summarised by Langfield-Smith and Greenwood (1998), Western business environments have traditionally not included life-long employment, face-to-face negotiation, co-ownership between buyers and sellers and sharing of career paths. This is, of course, an allusion to the Japanese principles on which the theories of fostering business relationships have evolved. Nonetheless, advantages of partnership, which include the avoidance of adversarial relationships, elimination of conflict, agreement on problem resolution, cost and time savings, necessitate its consideration as the premise for longevity which supports the move from a transactional model to a co-operative framework (Matthyssens and van den Bulte, 1994).

The KAM research emphasis is increasingly on the competences and skills required to successfully implement relational and key account management between buyers and sellers such as account selection and planning, processes to effective development, global management, reward, recruitment and selection mechanisms (refer, e.g., Cravens, Piercy and Shipp, 1996; Millman and Wilson, 1996; Blois, 1997; Boles et al., 1999; Hurcomb, 1999; Kempeners and van der Hart, 1999; Pardo, 1999;

Spencer, 1999; Millman, 1999; Weitz and Bradford, 1999; Schultz and Good, 2000; Walter and Gemunden, 2000; Holt and McDonald, 2001) while very little has been devoted to developing understanding of, particularly, the verbal exchange in buyer-seller communication (Schultz and Evans, 2002) or, specifically, negotiation (Millman and Wilson, 1998; Marsh 2000). Indeed, one practitioner, a director of IBM, has recently highlighted that a greater understanding communication enhances customer centricity (Mazur, 2003) while Walter and Gemunden (2000) consider negotiation, along with information exchange, to be crucial contributors to relational performance. Shaw (1999) notes there is a distinct lack of research in the area of inter-personal negotiating skills of buyers and sellers when the focus of the parties is longer term. Similar observations have also been made by Donaldson and O'Toole (2000) and Homburg, Workman and Jensen (2002), who call for a greater understanding of approaches and their relative successes.

Thus, relationships develop in a dynamic environment implying the relational task may be approached in different ways to achieve a desired outcome, which itself may vary according to the needs of the interacting organisations. Information exchange has been identified as having a pivotal role in the development of relationships. This is now found to be the focus of activity in industry as businesses attempt to compete in the marketplace by exploiting the information available to them. The literature highlights that face-to-face negotiation is seen to be an important core skill about which there is a clear need to develop a greater understanding, given the value-added relationships that many buyers and sellers are now engaged in.

Specifically, the objectives of this research were:

- to identify the nature of information exchange when buyers and sellers are engaged in longer-term relationships; and
- to explore the impact of information exchange on negotiation outcomes.

RESEARCH METHODOLOGY

The research comprised a multi-level, pluralistic design encompassing both qualitative and quantitative techniques in three mechanisms. This would enable the researcher to triangulate findings from different sources including the categorisation of relationships by stage of development. The research instruments comprised a mechanism for observation of negotiations i.e., the dominant research mechanism, plus semi-structured interviews and pre- and post-negotiation questionnaires. The unit of analysis was buyer-seller dyads (Iacobucci, 1996; Sekeran, 2000). Negotiations were viewed in this instance as critical when they are of key or strategic relevance to the parties (Yin, 1984). Secondary to this were preliminary interviews with key informants in both buying and selling organisations, and pre- and post-negotiation questionnaire instruments.

Extensive review of literature into negotiation and observation of interaction resulted in the development of a mutually exclusive content analytic coding mechanism with 36 categories of verbal behaviour under the headings of initiating, scene setting, reacting, specifying, clarifying and social (see Harwood, 2003). This tested highly reliable at Spearman .953.

The preliminary interviews comprised a series of questions to establish the dyadic relational development position and objectives for the meeting. Questionnaires were devised for all participants to determine any changes in attitudes and perceptions of participants following the negotiation and to understand the participants' views of its relative success, including level of commitment, risk-taking, flexibility, inclusion of tradable options and balance of power. An important consideration for the design of these instruments was their potential to introduce bias into the sample through influence of the participants' behaviour, particularly pre-negotiation. This issue would have been problematic if these mechanisms were the primary data collection method but triangulation was possible through analysis of both the content of negotiations and from key informant interviews (Mathews and Diamantopoulos, 1995). Nonetheless, for this reason it was decided not to use exactly the same questionnaire instrument at the pre-negotiation stage, rather to adopt a cut down version of the post-negotiation questionnaire.

A purposive sampling design was used (Patton, 1990) in order to test the observation mechanism and explore heterogeneity in negotiations of differing stages of relational development (Early, Mid and Partner) and, therefore, capture extremes of phenomena ie., the maximum range of variation (Guba and Lincoln, 1990; Maxwell, 1996). The sample comprised 12 dyads of completed data sets. This equated to 25 hours and 25 minutes of tape-recorded negotiation data (transcribed and coded into 13,406 units), 24 interviews, representing one for each buyer and seller partner, 22 sets of pre- and post-negotiation seller questionnaires and 12 sets of pre- and post-negotiation buyer questionnaires.

Analyses undertaken included statistical tests of independence (Pearson chi-square 462.010, df 70) for the observation data, based on relational stages identified as well as ratings for perceptions of outcome success, commitment, risk-taking, flexibility, inclusion of tradable options and balance of power. The latter analyses were conducted in order to explore the differences observed to be significant more closely.

ANALYSIS OF FINDINGS

At the Early stage, the observation data indicated much lower initiating (proposing and bargaining) behaviour as well as less specifying (identification of problems or needs and constraints). As anticipated, it was clear from this data that the role of the negotiation was to find out more information, both factual and personal, about the other party's position while limiting the range of issues on which they were prepared to reach agreement. It seems the range of issues were limited to those on which the parties had already undertaken preparatory work.

The Mid stage data demonstrated the long-term focus the parties had of their relationship with each other. Pre-negotiation data indicated they were the least happy with their preparation and planning for the negotiation, having the lowest perceptions of their skills and behaviours. After the negotiation, questionnaire data indicated the negotiation was more successful than that perceived at Early but less than Partner. The data suggested the parties had exchanged sufficient information to feel they had moved closer to the other party. Observation data indicated a lower level of information exchange on scene setting (positions) and reactions (emotive responses, including giving feelings, supporting and disagreeing) than Early and Partner stages. They engaged in considerably more initiating (proposing and bargaining) behaviour than the Early stage.

The Partner stage interview and questionnaire data indicated the closeness of the parties in their ratings of each other–they were more collaborative than the Early and Mid stages and considered the other party to be of high strategic importance. The data was clearly biased towards the longer-term focus (and future opportunities) the parties had for their relationship. The negotiation behaviour illustrated the parties exchanged the highest levels of scene setting and reacting, implying these are important aspects of the ongoing relationship. This stage also saw the highest levels of initiating behaviour although the relative level of tabling new issues indicated proposing focused on fewer options.

Nonetheless, the level of one initiating behaviour was observed to be almost three times greater than that in the Early stage, indicating their keenness to reach a satisfactory agreement.

The Partner stage saw the highest levels of specifying (identifying problems, implied or actual needs and constraints). Clarifying (testing and summarising) behaviour was observed to be higher than Early but lower than Mid. This indicates that such behaviours are necessary to reach a successful outcome in maintaining and building towards further relational development but that there is a fine balance in their optimal usage. Taken holistically, the data suggested that even though integrative in their overall behaviour, some competitive behaviour was used and, indeed, necessary in order to reach a satisfactory outcome.

Figure 1 illustrates the proportional levels (as a percentage) of behaviours observed in the data by relational stage, grouped into Early (based on 7,527 coded behaviours), Mid (2,757 behaviours) and Partner (3,202 behaviours) stages. Pearson chi-square analysis (in SPSS) indicated this was significant at 462,010 (df 70).

Figure 2 provides a more detailed view, based on groupings of the observation data by the Participants' ratings of, respectively, outcome success, commitment, flexibility, risk-taking, inclusion of tradable options and balance of power.

Where negotiations were rated as having a highly successful outcome (chi-square 224.210, df 25), so the levels of behaviours observed clearly indicated more initiating, specifying and less clarifying. A simi-

FIGURE 1. Observation Behaviours Grouped by Relational Stage (Early, Mid, Partner)

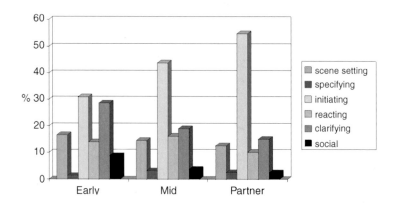

lar pattern is observed where the participants were committed to the outcome reached (chi-square 243.773, df 25), considered that flexibility during the negotiation was high (chi-square 233.350, df 25); and, to a lesser degree, the participants felt they had included the tradable options identified (chi-square 187.838, df 25). An inverse pattern, however, is observed for risk-taking during the negotiation (chi-square 114.728, df 25), whilst there is an increased level of reacting behaviour. Indeed, reacting is observed slightly more where outcome success, flexibility and inclusion of options is rated highly and slightly less where commitment is rated highly and power balance is evenly distributed (approximating a ratio of 50:50) (chi-square 144.532, df 25).

The chart illustrating balance of power (Figure 2 lower left) shows that clarifying is undertaken more where the parties perceived an imbalance in the power, while levels of initiating were similar. Social behaviours (giving and seeking information about personal matters) were observed at higher levels in less successful negotiations although where the balance of power was considered to be even, social and reacting behaviours appear to have been a contributing factor.

Particularly interesting in the data is the apparent perceptions of risk-taking and reacting which is surprising, given commentary in the literature on the need for creating additional value through greater customer centricity and relationships (eg., Mazur, 2003; Boles et al., 2000; Conway and Swift, 2000; Lapierre, 2000; Hogg et al., 1998), as it suggests the parties ascribed negative connotations to these behaviours. An explanation for this is that risk-taking is often considered to be adversarial (eg., Dawson, 1990), even though it is considered to achieve a more positive attitude to exploring new opportunities (Neale and Bazerman, 1991). Thus, there is a need for further investigation of this finding in the context of relational development. Moreover, Lamming and Caldwell (1999) suggest emotion is a considerable resource although de Burca (1999) argued that it may 'get in the way' of maintaining business relationships, detracting from their true purpose of strengthening competitiveness of the organisation by undermining rational decision-making. This, then, is also an area for further investigation.

CONCLUSIONS AND RECOMMENDATIONS

The findings provide a detailed understanding of face-to-face negotiation exchange between buyers and sellers engaged in relationship development. The results indicate distinct differences in the pattern of

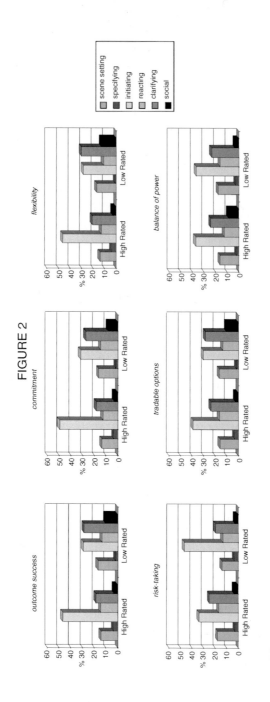

FIGURE 2

verbal exchange, strongly associated with relationship development. Thus, the factors considered in the negotiation literature to be important to the negotiation exchange process, specifically, outcome success, commitment, risk-taking, flexibility, inclusion of tradable options and balance of power, can be used to provide a means to measure the verbal exchange process. The analytical techniques used (and briefly described), therefore, provide a means to understanding how relationships proceed, albeit this research is a preliminary investigation. Furthermore, the differences observed may be used to manipulate verbal exchange in ways that improve the relational outcome, leading to greater customer satisfaction, as indicated by Keillor et al. (2000) and stronger 'glue' (Wilkinson and Young, 1994).

This calls for greater attention to the preparation and planning phase of negotiations, which is already emphasised by many authors in the field (eg., Lewicki et al., 1997). Clearly, this includes the history of relational exchanges between the parties, which is now increasingly focused on by organisations utilising RM technologies, in order to aid decision-making and maximise investments. The development of means by which to analyse and utilise information on relational exchanges in particular is, therefore, of paramount importance in managing quality at a more strategic level in relationships, as alluded to be Keillor et al. (2000).

Such an enhanced understanding enables the potential for extrapolation of the research mechanisms used to new settings. Marsh (2000) and de Burca (2001) highlight, however, the importance of recognising that every relationship is contextually different–it may be characterised by different actors with different priorities, preferences and styles of interaction (and hence provides researchers with problems of generalisable results). Thus, the approach requires further investigation in order to improve reliability and validity. Moreover, this paper reports on research which is strongly weighted on one data source, i.e., observation, albeit this is particularly strong evidence given the nature of the investigation. Future research should not only look to develop this aspect but also the additional methods, such as the pre- and post-negotiation questionnaires briefly reported on. Despite this, the findings of current research provides evidence on the nature of exchange, highlighting the need for appropriate skills in the strategic alignment of relationship management and development.

REFERENCES

Baiman, S., Rajan, M. V., and Kanodia, C. (2002). The role of information and opportunism in the choice of buyer-supplier relationships, Journal of Accounting Research, 40, 2, 247-287.

Ballantyne, D., Christopher, M., and Payne, A. (2000). Relationship Marketing: Bringing Quality, Customer Service and Marketing Together, Butterworth-Heinemann.

Bengtsson, M., and Kock, S. (1999). Cooperation and competition in relationships between competitors in business networks, The Journal of Business and Industrial Marketing, 14, 3, pp 178-194.

Blois, K. (1997). Are business-to-business relationships inherently unstable? Journal of Marketing Management, 13, pp 367-382.

Boles, J., Brashear, T., Bellenger, D., and Barksdale, H. Jnr (2000). Relationship selling behaviors: antecedents and relationship with performance, The Journal of Business & Industrial Marketing, 15, 2-3, pp 141-153.

Broderick, A. (1998). Role theory, relationship marketing and service performance, Proceedings of The Academy of Marketing Conference.

Burca de, S. (2001). Perceptions of the underlying dynamics in important business relationships, The Journal of Selling and Major Account Management, 2, 1, pp 31-63.

Burca de, S. (1999). Relationship practices in business markets: perceptions of stability, The Journal of Selling and Major Account Management, 2, 1, pp 31-63.

Caldwell, N., and Lamming, R. (1999). The case for including emotionality in sales and purchasing research, The Journal of Selling and Major Account Management, 1, 4, pp 33-46.

Carlisle, J. A., and Parker, R. C. (1989). Beyond Negotiation: Redeeming Customer-Supplier Relationships, Chichester: John Wiley and Sons, pp 35-36.

Cheverton, P. (1999). Key account management: the route to profitable key supplier status, London: Kogan Page Ltd.

Conway, T. and Swift, J. S. (2000). International relationship marketing: the importance of psychic distance, European Journal of Marketing, 34, 11/12, pp 1391-1413.

Cravens, D. W., Piercy, N. F., and Shipp, S. H. (1996). New organizational forms for competing in highly dynamic environments: the Network Paradigm, British Journal of Management, 7, pp 203-218.

Davenport, T. (1994). Saving IT's soul: human centred information management, Harvard Business Review, 72, March-April, pp 119-131.

Dawson, R. (1990). The Secrets of Power Negotiating, Chicago: Nightingale-Conant Corporation.

DeCormier, R., and Jobber, D. (1998). The Counsellor Selling Model: Components and Theory, The Journal of Selling and Major Account Management, 1, 2, pp 22-40.

Donaldson, B. (1996). Industrial Marketing Relationships and Open-to-Tender Contracts: Co-operation or Competition, Journal of Marketing Practice: Applied Marketing Science, 2, 2, pp 23-34.

Donaldson, B., and O'Toole, T. (2000). Classifying relationship structures: relationship strength in industrial markets, The Journal of Business and Industrial Marketing, 15, 7, pp 491-506.

Doughtery, V. (1999). Knowledge is about people, not databases, Industrial and Commercial Training, 31 (7), pp 262-266.

Dwyer, F. R., Schurr, P. H., and OH, S. (1987). Developing Buyer-Seller Relationships, Journal of Marketing, 51 (Apr), pp 11-27.

Ertel, D. (1999). Ideas at work: turning negotiation into a corporate capability, Harvard Business Review, May-June, pp 3-12.

Epinette, O., Petit, G. and Vialle, P. (1999). The role of interaction with key accounts in organizational learning: the Global One/Hewlett-Packard case, The Journal of Selling and Major Account Management, 2, 1, pp 64-87.

Fisher, R., and Ury, W. (1981). Getting to Yes, Boston: Houghton Mifflin.

Ford, D. (1997). Understanding Business Markets, 2nd Ed, London: Dryden.

Ford, D. (1990). Understanding Business Markets, London: Academic Press.

Ford, D. (1980). The development of buyer-seller relationships in industrial markets, European Journal of Marketing, 14 (5/6), pp 339-354.

Ford, D., Gadde, L-E., Håkansson, H., Lundgren, A., Snehota, I., Turnbull, P., and Wilson, D. (2000). Managing Business Relationships, Chichester: John Wiley & Sons.

Grönroos, C. (2001). Service Management and Marketing: A Customer Relationship Management Approach, 2nd Ed, London: Wiley.

Grönroos, C. (1997). Value-driven Relational Marketing: from Products to Resources and Competencies, Journal of Marketing Management, 13, pp 407-419.

Grönroos, C. (1996). Relationship marketing: strategic and tactical implications, Management Decision, 34-3, pp 5-14.

Grossman, R. P. (1998). Developing and managing effective consumer relationships, Journal of Product and Brand Management, 7, 1, pp 27-40.

Gummesson, E. (1994). Making relationship marketing operational, International Journal of Service Industry Management, 5, 5, pp 5-20.

Harwood, T. (2003). Negotiations in Buyer-Seller Relationships, unpublished PhD thesis, Leicester, De Montfort University.

Healy, M., Hastings, K., Brown, L., and Gardiner, M. (2001). The old, the new and the complicated: a trilogy of marketing relationships, European Journal of Marketing, 35, 1-2, pp 182-193.

Hendon, D. W., Henson, R. A., and Herbig, P. (1999). Cross-cultural business negotiations, Westport, CT: Praeger.

Hogg, M., Nutall, J., Long, G., and Davison, D. (1998). Relationship marketing: the challenge of operationalizing the components of relationship marketing, Proceedings of The Academy of Marketing Annual Conference, pp 628-629.

Holt, S. and McDonald, M. (2001). A boundary role theory perspective of the global account manager, The Journal of Selling and Major Account Management, 3, 4, pp 11-31.

Homburg, C., Workman, J. P. Jnr., and Jensen, O. (2002). A configurational perspective on key account management, Journal of Marketing, 66, 2, pp 38-60.

Hurcomb, J. (1999). Developing strategic customers and key accounts: the critical success factors, The Journal of Selling and Major Account Management, 1, 3, pp 49-59.

Huthwaite Research Group (1998). Negotiation skills trainer manual (unpublished), Rotherham: Huthwaite Research Group.

Hutt, M. D., Stafford, E. R., Walker, B. A., and Reingen, P. H. (2000). Case study: defining the social network of a strategic alliance, Sloan Management Review, 41, 2, pp 51-62.

Iacobucci, D., Ed (1996). Networks in Marketing, London: Sage Publications.

Keillor, B. D., Parker, R. S., and Pettijohn, C. E. (2000). Relationship-oriented characteristics and individual salesperson performance, The Journal of Business and Industrial Marketing, 15, 1, pp 7-22.

Kempeners, M. A., and Hart van der, H. W. (1999). Designing account management organizations, Journal of Business and Industrial Marketing, 14, 4, pp 310-327.

Lamming, R. (1993). Beyond partnership–strategies for innovation and lean supply, London: Prentice Hall.

Langfield-Smith, K., and Greenwood, M. R. (1998). Developing co-operative buyer-supplier relationships: a case study of Toyota, Journal of Management Studies, 35, 3 (May), pp 331-353.

Lapierre, J. (2000). Customer-perceived value in industrial contexts, The Journal of Business and Industrial Marketing, 15, 2-3, pp 122-140.

Lewicki, R. J., Saunders, D. M., and Minton, J. W. (1997). Essentials of Negotiation, Boston MA: Irwin McGraw-Hill.

Marsh, L. (2000). Relationship skills for strategic account management, The Journal of Selling and Major Account Management, 3, 1, pp 53-64.

Mathews, B. P., and Diamantopoulos, A. (1995). Response bias in executives' self-reports, Journal of Marketing Management, 11, pp 835-846.

Matthyssens, P., and Van den Bulte, C. (1994). Getting closer and nicer: partnerships in the supply chain, Long Range Planning, 27, 1, pp 72-83.

Mazur, L. (2003). Demanding change, Marketing Business, June, pp 12-14.

McDonald, M. (1998). Up close and personal, Marketing Business, Sept, pp 52-53.

McDonald, M., Millman, T., and Rogers, B. (1996). Key account management: learning from supplier and customer perspectives, Cranfield: The Centre for Advanced Research in Marketing at the Cranfield School of Management.

McDonald, M., Rogers, B., and Woodburn, D. (2000). Key Customers: How to Manage them Profitably, Oxford: Butterworth Heinneman.

Millman, A. F. (1994). Relational Aspects of Key Account Management, paper presented at the Fourth Seminar of the European Network for Project Marketing and Systems Selling, University of Pisa, Italy, 22/23 April.

Millman, A. F. (1999). From national account management to global account management in business-to-business markets, Thexis, 16, 4, pp 2-9.

Millman, A. F., and Wilson, K. J. (1998). Contentious issues in key account management, The Journal of Selling and Major Account Management, 1, 1, pp 27-37.

Millman, A. F., and Wilson, K. J. (1996). Developing key account management competences, Journal of Marketing Practice: Applied Marketing Science, 2, 2, pp7-22.

Millman, A. F., and Wilson, K. J. (1994). From Key Account Selling to Key Account Management, Tenth Annual Industrial Marketing and Purchasing (IMP) Conference, University of Groningen, The Netherlands, Sept.

Murray, J. S. (1986). Understanding Competing Theories of Negotiation, Negotiation Journal, 2 (Apr), pp 179-186.

Neale, M. A., and Bazerman, M. H. (1991). Cognition and Rationality in Negotiation, Oxford: Maxwell Macmillan International.

O'Toole, T., and Donaldson, B. (2000). Managing buyer-seller relationship archetypes, Irish Marketing Review, 13, 1, pp 12-20.

Pardo, C. (1999). Key account management in the business-to-business field: a French overview, Journal of Business and Industrial Marketing, 14, 4, pp 276-290.

Patton, M. Q. (1990). Qualitative evaluation and research methods 2nd ed, Newbury Park, CA: Sage.

Payne, A., and Frow, P. (1997). Relationship marketing: key issues for the utilities sector, Journal of Marketing Management, 13, pp 463-477.

Peters, L. D., and Fletcher, K. P. (1995). The role of trust in facilitating information exchange, Proceedings of the Annual Conference Making Marketing Work, Bradford: University of Bradford, II, pp 606-615.

Purdy, J. M., and Nye, P. (2000). The impact of communication media on negotiation outcomes, International Journal of Conflict Management, 11, 2, pp 162-187.

Rackham, N. (1987). Making Major Sales, Aldershot: Gower Publishing.

Raiffa, H. (1985). The Art and Science of Negotiation, Cambridge, MA: Harvard University Press.

Raiffa, H. (1997). Lectures on Negotiation Analysis, Cambridge MA: Program on Negotiation at Harvard Law School.

Reichheld, F. F., and Sasser, W. E. Jnr. (1990). Zero defections: quality comes to services, Harvard Business Review, Sept-Oct, pp 105-111.

Rich, M. K. (2000). The direction of marketing relationships, Journal of Business and Industrial Marketing, 15, 2/3, pp 170-179.

Rich, M. K., and Smith, D. C. (2000). Determining relationship skills of prospective salespeople, The Journal of Business and Industrial Marketing, 15, 4, pp 242-259.

Robinson, P. J., Faris, C. W., and Wind, Y. (1967). Industrial buying and creative marketing, Boston MA: Allyn and Bacon.

Schultz, R. J., and Evans, K. R. (2002). Strategic collaborative communication by key account representatives, The Journal of Personal Selling and Sales Management, 22, 1, pp 23-31.

Schultz, R. J., and Good, D. J. (2000). Impact of the consideration of future sales consequences and customer-oriented selling on long-term buyer-seller relationships, The Journal of Business and Industrial Marketing, 15, 4, pp 200-215.

Sekeran, U. (2000). Research methods for business 3rd ed, Chichester: Wiley.

Shaw, R. (1999). Book review, Journal of Targeting, Measurement and Analysis for Marketing, 8, 2, pp 199-200.

Sharma, N., and Patterson, P. G. (1999). The impact of communication effectiveness and service quality on relationship commitment in consumer, professional services, The Journal of Services Marketing, 13, 2, pp 151-170.

Spencer, R. (1999). Key accounts: effectively managing strategic complexity, Journal of Business and Industrial Marketing, 14, 4, pp 291-309.

Stern, L. W. (1996) Relationships, networks and the three Cs, in Iacobbuci D (1996), Networks in Marketing, London: Sage Publications.

Strong, E. K. (1925). The Psychology of Selling, New York: McGraw Hill.

Valley, K. (2000). The electronic negotiator, Harvard Business Review, Jan-Feb, pp 2-3.

Veloutsou, C., Saren, M., and Tzokas, N. (2002). Relationship marketing: what if ... ? European Journal of Marketing, 36, 4, pp 433-449.

Walter, A., and Gemunden, H. G. (2000). Bridging the gap between suppliers and customers through relationship promoters: theoretical considerations and empirical results, The Journal of Business & Industrial Marketing, 15, 2-3, pp 86-105.

Weitz, B. A., and Bradford, K. A. (1999). Personal selling and sales management: a relationship marketing perspective, Journal of the Academy of Marketing Sciences, 27, 2 pp 241-254.

Wilkinson, I. F., and Young, L. C. (1994). Working paper: Business dancing–understanding and managing interfirm relations, University of Western Sydney in conjunction with The Centre for International Management and Commerce.

Wilson, K. (1999). Developing Key Account Relationships: The Integration of the Millman-Wilson Relational Development Model with the Problem Centred (PPF) Model of Buyer-Seller Interaction in Business-to-Business Markets, The Journal of Selling and Major Account Management, 1, 3, pp 11-32.

Wren, B. M., and Simpson, J. T. (1996). A dyadic model of relationships in organizational buying: a synthesis of research results, Journal of Business and Industrial Marketing, 11, 3/4, pp 63-79.

Yin, R. K. (1984). Case study research: design and methods, Beverly Hills, CA: Sage.

Zineldin, M. Z. (2000). Total relationship management (TRM) and total quality management (TQM), Managerial Auditing Journal, 15, 1-2, pp 20-28.

Index

In this index, page numbers followed by the letter "f" designate figures; page numbers followed by the letter "t" designate tables.

BOOK ORDER FORM!

Order a copy of this book with this form or online at:
http://www.haworthpress.com/store/product.asp?sku= 5767

The Future of Relationship Marketing

____ in softbound at $19.95 ISBN-13: 978-0-7890-3162-4 / ISBN-10: 0-7890-3162-0.
____ in hardbound at $29.95 ISBN-13: 978-0-7890-3161-7 / ISBN-10: 0-7890-3161-2.

COST OF BOOKS _____

POSTAGE & HANDLING _____
US: $4.00 for first book & $1.50
for each additional book
Outside US: $5.00 for first book
& $2.00 for each additional book.

SUBTOTAL _____

In Canada: add 7% GST. _____

STATE TAX _____
CA, IL, IN, MN, NJ, NY, OH, PA & SD residents
please add appropriate local sales tax.

FINAL TOTAL _____
If paying in Canadian funds, convert
using the current exchange rate,
UNESCO coupons welcome.

❏ BILL ME LATER:
Bill-me option is good on US/Canada/
Mexico orders only; not good to jobbers,
wholesalers, or subscription agencies.

❏ Signature _____

❏ Payment Enclosed: $_____

❏ Please charge to my credit card:

❏ Visa ❏ MasterCard ❏ AmEx ❏ Discover
❏ Diner's Club ❏ Eurocard ❏ JCB

Account #_____

Exp Date _____

Signature_____
(Prices in US dollars and subject to change without notice.)

PLEASE PRINT ALL INFORMATION OR ATTACH YOUR BUSINESS CARD

Name	
Address	
City	State/Province	Zip/Postal Code
Country	
Tel	Fax

May we use your e-mail address for confirmations and other types of information? ❏ Yes ❏ No We appreciate receiving
your e-mail address. Haworth would like to e-mail special discount offers to you, as a preferred customer.
We will never share, rent, or exchange your e-mail address. We regard such actions as an invasion of your privacy.

Order from your **local bookstore** or directly from
The Haworth Press, Inc. 10 Alice Street, Binghamton, New York 13904-1580 • USA
Call our toll-free number (1-800-429-6784) / Outside US/Canada: (607) 722-5857
Fax: 1-800-895-0582 / Outside US/Canada: (607) 771-0012
E-mail your order to us: orders@haworthpress.com

For orders outside US and Canada, you may wish to order through your local
sales representative, distributor, or bookseller.
For information, see http://haworthpress.com/distributors

(Discounts are available for individual orders in US and Canada only, not booksellers/distributors.)

Please photocopy this form for your personal use.
www.HaworthPress.com   BOF06